Domain Names For Dummies®

Cheat

D0859042

How to Choose a Great Domain Name

- ✔ **Keep it short.** Names of less than 15 characters are best, because they're easy to remember and can be typed quickly.

- ✔ **Opt for something simple.** Complicated or obscure domain names are more likely to be forgotten.

- ✔ **Stay away from acronyms.** Unless the acronym you want to use is well known by the general public (or at least by the audience you intend to be using your Web site), avoid using it. Just because *you* know what the letters stand for doesn't mean your audience will.

- ✔ **Make the name memorable.** Try to choose a word that comes to mind easily when people think of your product, service, or topic.

- ✔ **Pick a name that is easy to pronounce and spell.** If you choose something that your audience may be likely to misspell, you run the risk that they may never make it to your site. Just to be sure you don't lose anyone, register potential misspellings in addition to the domain name of your choosing, so that if readers mistype your domain name, they'll still get to your site.

- ✔ **Find a name that's evocative.** A word that is associated with positive emotions is probably better than one that's associated with negative ones.

- ✔ **Avoid negative or offensive meanings in English as well as other languages.** If you plan to do business in non-English-speaking countries, check to be sure the name you're considering doesn't mean something negative or offensive in other languages.

Tips for Buying and Selling

- ✔ Keep copies of all documentation.

- ✔ Be sure to verify the accuracy of the domain name's registration information before you buy or sell.

- ✔ Make sure the domain name is free of trademark issues before you make an offer on it.

- ✔ Get your domain name appraised before you sell it.

- ✔ As a seller, do not set your expectations too high.

- ✔ Never let your domain name registration expire; if you do, you will not be able to sell your domain name.

Restricted-Use TLDs

- ✔ `.edu`: This TLD is reserved for four-year, degree-granting educational institutions in the United States.

- ✔ `.gov`: Only organizations and agencies of the United States government can use this TLD.

- ✔ `.int`: Organizations established by international treaties between governments, including some agencies and organizations of the United Nations, are the only ones allowed to use this TLD.

- ✔ `.mil`: The U.S. military is the lucky group that gets to claim this TLD as its own.

Domain Names For Dummies®

Cheat Sheet

The Cost of Registering Your Name

Registration Period	Price Range
1 year	$15–$35
2 years	$30–$70
3 years	$88–$105
5 years	$75–$175
10 years	$150–$350

The Newest TLDs

In November 2000, the Internet Corporation for Assigned Names and Numbers (ICANN) approved seven additional TLDs:

- ✔ .aero for the transport industry
- ✔ .biz for general use
- ✔ .coop for business cooperatives
- ✔ .info for general use
- ✔ .museum for museums
- ✔ .name for personal Internet addresses
- ✔ .pro for professionals, such as doctors and lawyers

Where to Turn for Trademark Information

- ✔ **The U.S. Patent and Trademark Office,** General Information Services Division, Crystal Plaza 3, Room 2C02, Washington, D.C. 20231; phone: 703-308-4357 or 800-786-9199 (toll-free); Web site: www.uspto.gov

- ✔ **The Sunnyvale Center on Innovation, Invention and Ideas,** 465 South Mathilda Avenue, Suite 300, Sunnyvale, CA 94086; phone: 408-730-7290; Web site: www.sci3.com

- ✔ **International Trademark Association (INTA),** 1133 Avenue of the Americas, New York, NY 10036; phone: 212-768-9887; Web site: www.inta.org

Hungry Minds™

For Dummies®: Bestselling Book Series for Beginners

 TM

...FOR DUMMIES

References for the Rest of Us!®

BESTSELLING BOOK SERIES

Are you intimidated and confused by computers? Do you find that traditional manuals are overloaded with technical details you'll never use? Do your friends and family always call you to fix simple problems on their PCs? Then the For Dummies® computer book series from Hungry Minds, Inc. is for you.

For Dummies books are written for those frustrated computer users who know they aren't really dumb but find that PC hardware, software, and indeed the unique vocabulary of computing make them feel helpless. For Dummies books use a lighthearted approach, a down-to-earth style, and even cartoons and humorous icons to dispel computer novices' fears and build their confidence. Lighthearted but not lightweight, these books are a perfect survival guide for anyone forced to use a computer.

> *"I like my copy so much I told friends; now they bought copies."*
> — *Irene C., Orwell, Ohio*

> *"Quick, concise, nontechnical, and humorous."*
> — *Jay A., Elburn, Illinois*

> *"Thanks, I needed this book. Now I can sleep at night."*
> — *Robin F., British Columbia, Canada*

Already, millions of satisfied readers agree. They have made For Dummies books the #1 introductory level computer book series and have written asking for more. So, if you're looking for the most fun and easy way to learn about computers, look to For Dummies books to give you a helping hand.

Hungry Minds™

Domain Names
FOR
DUMMIES®

by GreatDomains.com with Susan Wels

Foreword by Steve Newman

Hungry Minds™

HUNGRY MINDS, INC.

New York, NY ◆ Cleveland, OH ◆ Indianapolis, IN

TK5105
.875
.I57
G735
2001x

Domain Names For Dummies®

Published by:
Hungry Minds, Inc.
909 Third Avenue
New York, NY 10022
www.hungryminds.com
www.dummies.com

Library of Congress Control Number: 00111132

ISBN: 0-7645-5317-8

Printed in the United States of America

10 9 8 7 6 5 4 3 2 1

1B/QZ/QU/QR/IN

Distributed in the United States by Hungry Minds, Inc.

Distributed by CDG Books Canada Inc. for Canada; by Transworld Publishers Limited in the United Kingdom; by IDG Norge Books for Norway; by IDG Sweden Books for Sweden; by IDG Books Australia Publishing Corporation Pty. Ltd. for Australia and New Zealand; by TransQuest Publishers Pte Ltd. for Singapore, Malaysia, Thailand, Indonesia, and Hong Kong; by Gotop Information Inc. for Taiwan; by ICG Muse, Inc. for Japan; by Intersoft for South Africa; by Eyrolles for France; by International Thomson Publishing for Germany, Austria and Switzerland; by Distribuidora Cuspide for Argentina; by LR International for Brazil; by Galileo Libros for Chile; by Ediciones ZETA S.C.R. Ltda. for Peru; by WS Computer Publishing Corporation, Inc., for the Philippines; by Contemporanea de Ediciones for Venezuela; by Express Computer Distributors for the Caribbean and West Indies; by Micronesia Media Distributor, Inc. for Micronesia; by Chips Computadoras S.A. de C.V. for Mexico; by Editorial Norma de Panama S.A. for Panama; by American Bookshops for Finland.

For general information on Hungry Minds' products and services please contact our Customer Care department; within the U.S. at 800-762-2974, outside the U.S. at 317-572-3993 or fax 317-572-4002.

For sales inquiries and resellers information, including discounts, premium and bulk quantity sales and foreign language translations please contact our Customer Care department at 800-434-3422, fax 317-572-4002 or write to Hungry Minds, Inc., Attn: Customer Care department, 10475 Crosspoint Boulevard, Indianapolis, IN 46256.

For information on licensing foreign or domestic rights, please contact our Sub-Rights Customer Care department at 212-884-5000.

For information on using Hungry Minds' products and services in the classroom or for ordering examination copies, please contact our Educational Sales department at 800-434-2086 or fax 317-572-4005.

Please contact our Public Relations department at 212-884-5163 for press review copies or 212-884-5000 for author interviews and other publicity information or fax 212-884-5400.

For authorization to photocopy items for corporate, personal, or educational use, please contact Copyright Clearance Center, 222 Rosewood Drive, Danvers, MA 01923, or fax 978-750-4470.

Hungry Minds™ is a trademark of Hungry Minds, Inc.

About the Authors

Steve Newman, founder of GreatDomains.com, created with Jeff Tinsley and Irene Ing the first secondary market for domain names in 1996, early on recognizing a need for domain names to be brought to their highest and best use. In September 1999, GreatDomains.com was incorporated and Mr. Newman served as its Chairman and President until the widely noted sale in October 2000 to VeriSign, the leader in Internet Trust Services and a $30 billion public company. GreatDomains.com has been responsible for most of the high-profile domain names sold through a broker, including Drugs.com, Loans.com, and Cinema.com and is also known as the premier domain appraisal expert. Prior to GreatDomains.com, Mr. Newman was the Director of Finance for Nestle USA and co-founded Multimedia Realty, Inc., a California Real Estate Brokerage.

Susan Wels is a national best-selling author. Her books have included *Titanic: Legacy of the World's Greatest Ocean Liner, The Olympic Spirit: 100 Years of the Games, America: Then and Now,* and *Stanford: Portrait of a University.*

Authors' Acknowledgments

We are grateful for the help of Jonathan Barsade, Sean Downey, Kirk Feldhus, and Wuang-Ee Blum at GreatDomains.com. We also thank Mark McGuire of NameProtect and Chris deMassa of Trademark Express for their valuable assistance.

Publisher's Acknowledgments

We're proud of this book; please send us your comments through our Online Registration Form located at www.dummies.com.

Some of the people who helped bring this book to market include the following:

Acquisitions, Editorial, and Media Development

Project Editor: Elizabeth Netedu Kuball

Acquisitions Editor: Jonathan Malysiak

Acquisitions Coordinator: Lauren Cundiff

Technical Editors: Jonathan Barsade, R.T. Griffiths, and Matthew McClure

Senior Permissions Editor: Carmen Krikorian

Editorial Manager: Pamela Mourouzis

Editorial Administrator: Michelle Hacker

Production

Project Coordinator: Regina Snyder

Layout and Graphics: Amy Adrian, John Greenough, Jackie Nicholas, Jacque Schneider, Rashell Smith, Julie Trippetti, Jeremey Unger

Proofreaders: Valery Bourke, Angel Perez, York Production Services, Inc.

Indexer: York Production Services, Inc.

General and Administrative

Hungry Minds, Inc.: John Kilcullen, CEO; Bill Barry, President and COO; John Ball, Executive VP, Operations & Administration; John Harris, CFO

Hungry Minds Consumer Reference Group

Business: Kathleen Nebenhaus, Vice President and Publisher; Kevin Thornton, Acquisitions Manager

Cooking/Gardening: Jennifer Feldman, Associate Vice President and Publisher; Anne Ficklen, Executive Editor

Education/Reference: Diane Graves Steele, Vice President and Publisher; Greg Tubach, Publishing Director

Lifestyles: Kathleen Nebenhaus, Vice President and Publisher; Tracy Boggier, Managing Editor

Pets: Dominique De Vito, Associate Vice President and Publisher; Tracy Boggier, Managing Editor

Travel: Michael Spring, Vice President and Publisher; Brice Gosnell, Publishing Director; Suzanne Jannetta, Editorial Director

Hungry Minds Consumer Editorial Services: Kathleen Nebenhaus, Vice President and Publisher; Kristin A. Cocks, Editorial Director; Cindy Kitchel, Editorial Director

Hungry Minds Consumer Production: Debbie Stailey, Production Director

◆

The publisher would like to give special thanks to Patrick J. McGovern, without whom this book would not have been possible.

◆

Contents at a Glance

Cartoons at a Glance

By Rich Tennant

"I'm sorry Mr. Garret, a 35 year old tattoo doesn't qualify as a legal trademark for 'Mother.com'."

page 57

"The divorce was amicable. She got the Jetta, the sailboat and the recumbent bike. I got the servers and the domain name."

page 7

"Hey–here's a company that develops short memorable domain names for new businesses. It's listed at www.CompanyThatDevelopsShort-MemorableDomainNamesForNewBusinesees.com."

page 37

page 191

"I'm sorry, but 'Arf', 'Bark', and 'Woof' are already registered domain names. How about 'Oink', 'Quack', or 'Moo'?"

page 99

"I assume you'll be forward thinking enough to allow '.dog' as a valid domain name."

page 145

page 125

Cartoon Information:
Fax: 978-546-7747
E-Mail: richtennant@the5thwave.com
World Wide Web: www.the5thwave.com

Table of Contents

Foreword

⁌he greatest land grab in the history of the world is occurring as we speak. But it's not physical land that is up for grabs; it's the land of the new economy — domain names, or Web site addresses — that have become the world's new prized commodities.

With recent publicized domain name sales such as Loans.com for $3 million dollars and Business.com for $7.5 million dollars, ordinary individuals have become domain name millionaires overnight.

But with more than 20 million domain names now in existence, most domain names are not million-dollar names. Thousands of names are registered each day online at registrars such as Network Solutions for $35 dollars annually and on the emerging secondary market at sites such as GreatDomains.com for as little as $250 for a previously-registered name.

Buying a domain name is only the beginning. With strong laws on domain name cybersquatting and trademark rights, owners of domain names must take active steps to protect their valuable virtual real estate and ensure that it doesn't infringe on the rights of third parties, lest they risk losing their domain names.

In unique clarity, by reading this book you will discover how to:

- Acquire the perfect domain names for your business or personal use.
- Determine how much to pay for your domain names.
- Sell domain names using techniques of the "domain name millionaires."
- Take steps to protect your investment in your domain name.
- Buy and sell fully-developed Web sites.

Taking the time to read this educational and entertaining look at domain names may prove to be your wisest decision on your path to Internet homesteading.

I sincerely wish you much success and good luck in finding your perfect domain name!

Steve Newman

Founder, GreatDomains.com

Introduction

The Internet isn't the next wave. It's already here, roaring unstoppably through every sector of our economy. Today, less than a decade after the birth of the World Wide Web, more than 160 million people around the world are on the Net — nearly 120 million of them in the U.S. alone — and the global Internet community will include more than half a billion people by 2003. "It took radio more than 30 years to reach 60 million people, and television 15 years," *Business Week* commented recently. Never has a technology taken off around the world so fast as the Internet has. All over the world, millions of companies, organizations, and individuals are scrambling to get a place on board.

For every one of them, the ticket to the Internet is the domain name. These online addresses — like Amazon.com — are the point of entry to the world-wide electronic marketplace. A domain name is the equivalent of Internet real estate — a place or address where you can receive mail or build a home page, an online store, a virtual library, or anything else you could possibly imagine.

As a result, the demand for domain names has been soaring. In 1995, only 100,000 domain names had been registered. By the end of 2000, the number had rocketed to around 12 million, and according to some estimates, there will be 140 million registered domain names by 2003.

About This Book

This book is designed to help you navigate the virtual world of acquiring, buying, and selling domain names. It covers all the basics — how to find the best domain name for your purposes, how to figure out if it's available, how to buy or sell a name on the resale market, and how to determine whether the price is right. And it includes the most up-to-date information on the brand new domain name suffixes that have just been approved as supplements to the standard `.com`, `.net`, and `.org` choices.

The information that you'll find inside this book draws on the extensive knowledge of Steve Newman and his team at GreatDomains.com, the Internet's premiere domain name reseller. In this book, we provide valuable "insider" tips based on our years of domain name experience.

We also offer some up-to-the-minute advice on the brand-new business of buying and selling developed Web sites or Web businesses — which is likely to be the next wave in the Internet marketplace. In addition, we walk you through the ins and outs of domain name trademark issues, a topic that is especially important for anyone who plans to use his domain name in business.

Of course, we don't expect you to read this book from cover to cover. Instead, just dip in to find the tips you need. Whatever domain name question interests you, turn right to that section for the information you need.

Foolish Assumptions

Although the Internet once belonged almost exclusively to computer techies, it is now the playground of millions of ordinary people of all ages and backgrounds. As a result, the only skill you need to register, buy, or sell a domain name is the ability to use a computer and get online.

Whenever we use a technical term in this book, we tell you what it means. And we take you step-by-step through any relatively complicated procedure. So whether you've been surfing the Net since its inception or you're just paddling out for the first time with your board in tow, you'll find the answers you need to be hanging ten in no time.

How This Book Is Organized

This book is divided into eight parts. Each one deals with a different type of process or issue relating to domain names, the market for them, trademark conflicts, and the brand-new market for Web sites.

Part 1: Understanding Domain Names

In this section, you find all the basics. We explain how domain names work and take you on a very brief and non-sleep-inducing tour of the Internet's history. You get a guide to domain name and Internet address components, from the www to the .com. And you meet some folks who have turned their virtual domain name real estate into very profitable investments.

Part II: Finding the Right Domain Name

Are you ready to get a domain name of your own? In the chapters in this part, we show you how to get started. In this section, you find out what you need to know to pick the best possible domain name for your purposes, see if it's available, and register it from your choice of the dozens of registrars. We give you information on everything from choosing the right domain name suffix (like .com or .net) to various registration costs and features.

Part III: Navigating the Sometimes Rough Waters of Trademark Issues

Domain name trademark issues have become increasingly important as more and more businesses get on the Net and aggressively protect their marks and brands. In this section, we explain key steps you need to take to protect your domain name from potential trademark conflicts. You get information on everything from cybersquatting to domain name dispute resolution and how to apply for a federal trademark for your domain name.

Part IV: Buying a Domain Name

A great domain name can be hard to find, especially since so many have already been registered. But even if you strike out when you try to find the perfect "unused" domain name, you can still find a great name on the resale market. In this section, you find out what you need to know to buy domain names successfully. We also provide a valuation method to help you make sure that you're paying the right price.

Part V: Profiting from Your Domain Name

There is gold in the Internet land rush, and many people have already cashed in through the domain name resale market and other opportunities. This section gives you tips on how to sell your domain name successfully — whether you choose to sell it yourself, use the services of a domain name broker, or put it up for bid at an online auction site.

Part VI: Buying and Selling Web Sites

As the Internet matures, the next wave may be the Web site resale market. This part gives you the basics you need to know about strategies for buying, valuing, and selling Web-based businesses.

Part VII: The Part of Tens

Here you find short bursts of information that answer lots of your domain name questions — everything from resale prices to which Web sites are the best. We also cover the do's and don'ts of registering, buying, selling, and protecting your domain name in this handy little part.

Appendixes:

In this part of the book, we put together some extras to help you make the most of your domain name experience. Appendix A gives you the list of the country-code domain name suffixes (like `.uk` for the United Kingdom and `.fr` for France), with contact information for each country. Appendix B is a glossary of technical terms that you will find inside this book. Appendix C is a list of online resources and links that you may find especially helpful, organized according to topic.

Icons Used in This Book

Icons are those little pictures you see in the margins throughout the following pages, and this wouldn't be a . . . *For Dummies* book without them. The purpose of those icons is to grab your attention for a particular reason. Here's a list of the icons we use in this book, along with explanations of what information they highlight:

Whenever you see this icon, you're sure to find important information on legal cases related to domain name trademark conflicts.

This bull's-eye gets right to the point, highlighting especially helpful ideas and providing you with suggestions for ways you can do things better.

This icon, just like a piece of string tied to your finger, serves as a reminder that you should be sure to keep in mind the information nearby.

Whenever you see this icon, you'll find important information on situations that could potentially cause you problems, along with suggestions for ways to avoid them.

This icons marks information that could interest you — or that you may want to skip and come back to later on. If you're in a hurry and just want to get the basics, you can skip the paragraphs with this icon and know that you're not missing anything critical to your understanding of the topic at hand.

Where to Go from Here

Ready to get started? Just pick whichever section you're interested in and get going. If you want to know the basics about registering domain names, Parts I and II are the best places to start. If you're thinking about buying or selling domain names, you may want to flip directly to Parts IV and V. And if you have trademark questions, you can find many of your answers in Part III. So what are you waiting for?

Part I
Understanding Domain Names

The 5th Wave   By Rich Tennant

"The divorce was amicable. She got the Jetta, the sailboat and the recumbent bike. I got the servers and the domain name."

In this part . . .

The chapters in this part are a great place to start, whether you're new to the world of domain names or you just want to refresh your memory about the importance of domain names in the world today. Here you'll find information on the buying and selling of domain names — and what a hot commodity they've become! We also break down domain names into their various parts, so you can talk like a pro when you're negotiating a sale. Finally, we let you know about some people who've blazed the trail in the world of domain names, making big profits on their purchases. Looking for a place to start? You found it!

Chapter 1

The New Domain Name Marketplace

*J*ust a few years ago — before our world changed forever with the emergence of the Internet, the World Wide Web, e-mail, and electronic commerce — people depended on traditional tools for running their businesses and communicating with customers, suppliers, family, and friends. If you were starting a business, the bottom-line basics you needed certainly included a street or mailing address, a telephone number, and a box of business cards. To communicate with someone, you'd either pick up the phone, write a letter, or maybe, if you were in a hurry, send a fax.

But all that, of course, has changed radically. Today, in addition to a physical location, almost every business needs an Internet location, too — a site or address on the Net where customers can find you, learn about your products and services, communicate with you through electronic mail, and maybe place electronic orders. These Internet addresses — for example, Myfirmname.com — are called *domain names*. They are the keys that give you entry to the worldwide electronic marketplace and the vast communications network of the Internet.

Domain names, though, are not just for businesses or organizations. Today, more and more individuals want their own domain names, too — for e-mail addresses with extra impact and personal Web sites that help them share their interests, enthusiasms, and expertise with others.

In this chapter, we explore what domain names are and why having a domain name is increasingly important to so many individuals and businesses. We give you a brief background on how the Internet domain name system works, look ahead at future trends, and show you the first steps to take to get a domain name of your own.

What Is a Domain Name?

Once upon a time, the Internet was a brave new world inhabited only by academics, scientists, and people who worked for obscure government agencies. Beginning in those early days, every computer that was hooked up to the Internet was assigned a unique identity code. This code, called an *Internet Protocol* (IP) address, is a string of numbers like 24.187.906. IP addresses enable computers to transmit information to precise destinations over the Internet — just as your phone number allows your family and friends to reach you in your house, and your zip code is specific to your town or area of town.

The IP address system was great for the small community of techies who launched the Internet (believe it or not, there were only about 1,000 computers connected to the Net back in 1984, when the Internet was very young). But as the Internet began to grow and more nontechnical people began to use it, the numerical IP address system began to have increasing drawbacks. For one thing, those long strings of numbers were difficult to remember, and they could be off-putting for people who weren't technically inclined.

Fortunately, that same year — 1984 — the much easier-to-use domain name system was created. Domain names are word-based Internet addresses, such as Myfirmname.com. Basically, every domain name is an alias for a numerical IP code. For instance, the domain name GreatDomains.com actually serves as an alias for the IP address 207.171.0.9. Computers on the Internet automatically translate domain names into the corresponding numerical IP addresses. Then your computer can transmit information to the computer that has the specific IP address you're trying to reach.

The domain name system has made the global network of the Internet much simpler to navigate, because words are a lot easier to remember than long, coded strings of numbers. But words also have a lot of associated images and meanings — which is why, over the last decade, domain names have turned into much more than mere Internet addresses. The best of them, such as Amazon.com, have emerged as powerful brand names, corporate identities, and prestigious locations on the information highway.

Who Needs a Domain Name?

Anyone who wants to have his own location on the Internet needs a domain name. In effect, a domain name is your own little piece of Internet real estate.

A domain name is a virtual address that you can use for sending or receiving information — and a cyberspace location that you can develop into anything from the simplest homemade Web page to the most sophisticatedly designed e-commerce site.

If you fit into any of the following categories, having a domain name probably makes sense for you:

- ✔ **You have an existing organization or business, and you want to market your products or services over the Internet.** More and more traditional businesses are realizing that they need to have a presence on the Internet if they want to reach and keep their customers. After all, people are increasingly turning to the Net for products and information — and if they don't find your business on the Web, there's a good chance that they'll find one or more of your competitors. Organizations, too, risk seeming behind-the-times if they don't take advantage of the easy access of the Net to post and share information that's vital to their members or constituents.

- ✔ **You want to start a brand-new business.** In some ways, thanks to the Internet, starting a business has never been easier. Anyone with a telephone line and a computer now has instant access to a worldwide marketplace. Plus, with the right domain name, you can attract customers to your products and services with relatively little marketing expense (for more information on choosing the right domain name, turn to Chapter 4). And a growing range of low-cost Internet business tools, such as e-commerce packages, can help you rapidly set up your business.

   Of course, launching a successful enterprise involves a lot more than having the right domain name and Web site — far more than we could ever attempt to deal with in this book. But the Internet has made it much easier for entrepreneurs to get started, and getting a domain name is one of the first and most important steps to take.

- ✔ **You're an independent freelancer or consultant.** By obtaining a domain name and setting up an informative Web site, consultants and freelancers can create a virtual brochure that highlights their services and skills — with a worldwide reach and at a fraction of the cost of printed marketing materials.

- ✔ **You have an interest or passion that you'd like to share with others.** Whether you want to share your knowledge of 19th-century riveting techniques, document your family history, or start a group for people who share similar interests and concerns, having a domain name and a Web site can give you access to a larger community and audience than was ever possible before.

- ✔ **You want a personal stake in the Internet.** For some individuals, having a domain name and perhaps their own personal Web page is an identity statement — a declaration that they're part of the Internet age. Other individuals — seeing that domain names have increased rapidly in value —

decide to acquire one or more domain names so they will have a financial stake in the future of the Internet marketplace.

This type of investment should only be considered if the domain name(s) you are interested in acquiring do not infringe on any existing trademarks or other third-party rights (we cover a lot more about domain name trademark issues in Part III of this book).

What Can You Do with a Domain Name?

More than anything, a domain name can help give you a recognizable identity on the Internet, opening up a world of personal and business opportunity. The following sections list some of the most common uses for domain names.

Use it as part of your e-mail address

Many domain name services make it easy for you to use your domain name as your e-mail address. Using a domain name this way can give you a much more distinctive or professional Internet presence. For example, an e-mail address like myname@myfirmname.com can convey a more polished and put-together image than myname@myInternetServiceProvidersaddress.com. Using your business domain name as your e-mail address is also an easy way to remind people of your business or organization's identity — instead of advertising the name of your Internet Service Provider (ISP) — every time that you communicate online.

Use it to build your own Web site

Domain name services also make it easy to link your domain name to a Web site, and many of them provide simple tools that you can use to create and post a Web site of your own (we cover more about those services in Chapter 5).

Use it to brand your business

The best domain names — think of Amazon.com — can also be built into powerful brand names. Of course, most people don't have the marketing budget to make their domain name a household word. But it's a fact that a memorable domain name can add instant marketing cachet to a product or service.

Use it as an investment

Ever since the Internet took off, people have been acquiring domain names as investments. In the early days, however, many of these speculators were *cybersquatters* — people who deliberately obtained domain names, like MTV.com, that they knew would be sought after by celebrities or major corporations. In effect, these individuals were holding the domain names hostage, hoping to profit by reselling them at high prices to their rightful trademark owners.

But the legal system is now catching up with cybersquatters. In 1999, Congress passed the Trademark Cyberpiracy Prevention Act, which makes it illegal for individuals to buy domain names in bad faith that deliberately infringe on trademarks that belong to others (we explore some details of these issues in Part III).

People who want to invest legitimately in domain names, especially generic names that don't have trademark issues, still have plenty of opportunities to do so. The domain name resale market, in fact, is booming (and we explore it further in Chapter 9). Good-faith domain name investors focus on generic names — such as Ebusiness.com — or memorable phrases that don't have trademark conflicts. Many people have reaped significant profits from this strategy (turn to Chapter 3 for some real-life examples).

How Does the Domain Name System Work?

The domain name system functions a lot like the postal system. It labels every piece of information sent through the Internet with the exact address of its destination computer, as well as the "return address" of the sender.

To understand the basics of the domain name system, it helps to know a little about the Internet — what it is and how it was developed.

A yawn-free history of the Internet

Today, it's nearly impossible to imagine the world without the Internet. Like the railroads, the radio, the telegraph, and the phone, the Net has revolutionized the way we see and interact with the world. It has changed how we communicate with each other and vastly expanded the boundaries of our daily lives. Unlike many groundbreaking inventions like the telephone and electric light, however, the Internet was not the brainchild of a single individual.

Instead, it developed over time as the result of long-term collaborations among experts in government agencies, academic institutions, and industry.

The Internet actually has its roots back in the late 1950s, when the U.S. government was alarmed by the Soviet Union's launch of the *Sputnik* satellite and the Soviets' apparent technological edge. To help bolster America's science and defense capabilities, the United States Department of Defense created the Advanced Research Projects Agency (ARPA). The head of the agency's computer research program was a scientist from the Massachusetts Institute of Technology (MIT) named J.C.R. Licklider. In 1962, before heading the program, Licklider wrote up his visionary idea for a "Galactic Network" made up of computers that would be linked to each other around the world.

Three years later, scientists at MIT and the University of California, Berkeley, succeeded for the first time in getting two computers on opposite sides of the country to "talk" to each other over a telephone line — one of the very first milestones in Internet history. Back in those days, though, the fledgling network was called the ARPANET, and in 1969 it had a grand total of four computers connected to it.

An "indestructible" network

The main reason the government was interested in building the ARPANET was for defense. Military planners wanted to create some kind of a secure command and control communications network that could survive a huge disaster like a nuclear attack. Decentralization, they realized, had to be a central feature of the system. The network needed to be so spread out and flexible that it could function even if some parts of it were totally destroyed.

For that reason, they decided not to set up the network like the long-distance phone system, which at the time routed calls through potentially vulnerable central hubs. Instead, they developed the ARPANET more on the model of the decentralized road and highway system, which offers multiple routes for getting to any particular point. If one pathway is blocked or slow, traffic can easily travel to its destination over another route.

Network planners adopted other innovations to keep electronic traffic flowing as smoothly as possible over the ARPANET, bypassing any potential obstacles. Instead of linking communicating computers with direct, dedicated connections through which entire, lengthy messages would pass, they created a system in which electronic messages were broken up into discrete little *packets* of information, like individual pieces of a jigsaw puzzle. Each piece or packet is labeled with the electronic IP addresses of the sending and receiving computers. Then it is sent out independently into the network and travels separately along its own pathway to the destination.

Inventing the World Wide Web

The Internet was created to be a *physical* "network of computer networks." On the Net, packets of electronic information are routed, through real-world computers and telecommunication lines, to their destinations. The World Wide Web, on the other hand, is a *virtual* network of documents and information connected, not by physical wires and cables, but by a computer language called *HTML.* This graphical language enables users to point, click, and jump from one document, or Web site, to another using *hypertext links* (coded connections between documents on the Web) — thereby navigating and exploring the infinitely rich information resources of the Net.

The idea for the World Wide Web was the brainstorm of a software engineer named Tim Berners-Lee. In 1989, Berners-Lee was working at CERN, the European Laboratory for Particle Physics in Geneva, Switzerland. His goal was to develop an easier way for Internet users to access all the available types of data and documentation on the Net. In 1990, Berners-Lee created the HTML computer language and developed a method for giving documents or Web pages their own Internet addresses (called *URLs,* short for *Uniform Resource Locators,* and covered in more detail in Chapter 2). He also invented a way to connect Web pages into a network of sites on the Internet (using a system called *HyperText Transfer Protocol,* or HTTP, which locates and automatically retrieves Web pages for viewing) as well as a program for browsing and finding information on his newly created World Wide Web. By the end of 1992, its second year of existence, there were only 50 sites on the fledgling Web; four years later, there were 40 million sites, and Internet traffic had increased a staggering 341,634 percent.

When all the packets arrive at the specified address, the system instantly reassembles them in the correct order. This innovation, called *packet switching,* gives the network enormous flexibility, because there are no dedicated routes that can get backed up or clogged by lengthy messages. Moreover, if any of the packets experiences a problem during transmission, that packet can be individually resent, so the entire message doesn't have to be retransmitted.

By 1972, 23 computers were connected to each other through the ARPANET, and similar networks were being developed in other parts of the U.S. and the world. It was becoming increasingly clear that there could someday be enormous nondefense uses for a technology that could link researchers and computer users in many different networks around the globe.

From ARPANET to Internet

In 1974, an important development helped network developers realize Licklider's vision of a "Galactic Network." Researchers developed a common language that enabled different, far-flung networks of computers to communicate with each other. Known as *TCP/IP* (which is short for the mouthful *Transmission Control Protocol/Internet Protocol*), this language was adopted by the ARPANET in 1982, and it quickly became the standard language used by computer networks. When all of these networks started communicating with each other using a common language, the Internet — literally "a network of networks" — was born.

One of the Internet's first major uses was electronic mail. The very first e-mail message — "Testing 1-2-3" — was transmitted in 1971, and in 1973, e-mail was already making up 75 percent of all transmissions over the ARPANET. In 1982, the word *Internet* was used for the very first time. And by the mid-1980s, when desktop PCs became commonplace, it was already in wide use for everyday communication, and other applications were rapidly coming into use, including file transfer, newsgroups, bulletin boards, and remote computer access.

Although the government and academics were continuing to spearhead the Internet's use and growth, it was also increasingly being used for commercial purposes. In 1989, for the first time, more than 100,000 computers were connected to the Internet around the world, and the number skyrocketed to 300,000 only a year later. Today, the Internet is a global information and commercial exchange linking millions of computers, networks, businesses, and individuals.

The domain name system

In the early 1980s, Paul Mockapetris of the University of Southern California invented the domain name system (DNS). He developed it as a way to make Internet addressing easier to manage as the number of users grew. In addition to introducing word-based domain names as aliases for numerical IP codes, the system created a number of domain name suffixes — called *extensions* or *top-level domains* (TLDs) — to be used as categories for U.S. Internet addresses. These TLDs included:

- ✔ .edu (for educational users)
- ✔ .com (for commercial users)
- ✔ .gov (for governmental users)
- ✔ .org (for international organizations)

The system also specified special country-code suffixes, called *ccTLDs,* for every nation that wished to issue domain names. (For more on TLDs, turn to Chapter 2.)

The domain name system plays a key role in the smooth operation of the Internet. It works so instantly and transparently, however, that most people aren't even aware of its existence. The DNS works behind the scenes something like this:

1. **When you type a domain name, like Businessname.org, into your browser bar, your computer automatically contacts another machine on the Net — called a *DNS server* or *name server* — and asks it for the domain name's corresponding IP code.**

2. **Your computer then transmits that IP code to another machine on the Internet called a *router*.**

3. **The router sends the data out over the Internet, through a variety of telecommunications lines and pathways, to the destination address computer you've specified.**

The process works in a matter of split seconds, usually without a hitch. Thanks to the domain name system, you can get instant access to millions of computers on the Internet — and for the most part, you only need to be able to type and spell.

Who Is in Charge of the Domain Name System?

Since the domain name system was invented in the 1980s, its management and administration have moved from a partnership of the government and academics in the U.S. to the international and commercial arena, reflecting the enormous global growth of the system. Along the way, however, continuing controversies and changes have occurred.

Originally, the administrator of the entire Internet IP addressing system, called the Internet Assigned Numbers Authority, was a single individual — a scientist named Jon Postel who worked at the Information Sciences Institute at the University of Southern California. This setup made sense in the early days, when the Internet was known for its informal, cooperative spirit.

As commercial uses of the Internet began to grow, however, this type of oversight structure became less satisfactory. After all, immense amounts of money were coming into play on the Net, so it seemed prudent to develop an administrative structure that had more formalized accountability and legal protections.

From public to private

In 1986, the National Science Foundation (NSF), a U.S. government agency, took over responsibility for the Internet, and in 1991 the NSF began overseeing the domain name registration system. The next year, a company called Network Solutions, Inc. (NSI), located in Herndon, Virginia, applied for an NSF contract to provide domain name registration services to the public. In 1993, through a cooperative agreement with the federal government, NSI won exclusive rights to control and administer the .com, .org, .net, and .edu TLDs in the United States.

Back in those days, this agreement did not represent a big-business deal for NSI. The U.S. government was still picking up the tab for domain names, and the few businesses that wanted to register .com domain names did so for free, courtesy of American taxpayers. The government simply compensated Network Solutions for its services on a cost-plus basis.

But in 1995, all that changed. That year, the government decided to stop subsidizing commercial domain names. It gave NSI the authority to charge $100 for .com registrations, plus an annual $50 fee to renew and maintain the registrations. Of course, the fees didn't stop a growing tidal wave of businesses from registering domain names. In 1993, there were 8,700 registered domain names; by March 1996, the figure was 315,000. And even though NSI contributed 30 percent of the fees it collected to a special Internet improvement fund, the cooperative agreement's profitability potential had changed dramatically.

Over time, the demand for domain names grew as the Internet attracted more users. The government's agreement with NSI to build a commercial domain name system was a success. So, in 1997, the National Science Foundation declared that it would not renew its 5-year-old agreement with NSI on an exclusive basis. Instead, it would open up domain name registrations to competition.

ICANN steps in

The next year, Internet godfather Jon Postel proposed a new, private, nonprofit, international corporation that would take on responsibility for managing the domain name system. Called the Internet Corporation for Assigned Names and Numbers (ICANN), the organization was authorized by the federal government in order to shift control of the Internet from the U.S. government to the international Internet community. One of ICANN's top priorities was to open up the domain name registration business to competition.

In November 1999, ICANN approved new rules under which domain name registration services for .com, .net, and .org TLDs would be provided by dozens of companies worldwide.

At the same time, however, Network Solutions would continue to administer the master databases that keep track of all available .com, .net, and .org domain names. In effect, NSI would wholesale domain names in those TLD categories to registration "retailers" who would provide services to the public around the world.

What else is ICANN up to?

ICANN has also been working on a dispute-resolution policy for domain name trademark conflicts. In August 1999, the group adopted a uniform dispute resolution policy for all ICANN-accredited registrars of .com, .net, and .org TLDs (for more information, see Chapter 6).

In November 2000, ICANN members voted to increase the number of TLDs to include seven brand new domain name suffixes: .aero, .biz, .coop, .info, .museum, .name, and .pro. The creation of new TLDs has been a controversial issue. Many people believe that creating new domain name suffixes will increase consumer choice and relieve the growing shortage of domain names. Others, however, believe that new TLDs will only increase the likelihood of consumer confusion and infringement of trademarks. Only time will tell.

Under the new process, *registrars* are the "retail" companies that handle all consumer contact for domain name registrations, including customer services and billing. *Registry administrators* are the "wholesale" organizations around the world (including Network Solutions for .com, .net, and .org) that maintain the master databases (called *root servers*) of all available domain names.

Today, as a result of competition, more than 80 accredited domain name registrars providing services exist around the world for .com, .net, and .org domain name registration. (For a complete list of ICANN-accredited registrars around the world, go to www.icann.org/registrars/accredited-list.html.)

Chapter 2

Parts Is Parts: Understanding the Syntax of Internet Addresses

*E*ven if you have already decided that you need a domain name, chances are that you may not have a clear idea what a domain name really is and how it fits into the ever-present strings of computer codes that we see on the Internet, such as `www.whatsthisallabout.com`.

In this chapter, we throw a little light on the subject, looking at all the pieces of a typical Internet address so that you'll know more about what's involved. After all, knowledge is power, and the more you understand, the more informed your choices will be when you choose a domain name of your own.

The World of the URL: Understanding Internet Addresses

Simply put, a domain name is part of an Internet address. Most of the time, you see these Internet addresses — called *URLs* (short for Uniform Resource Locators) — in the location bars at the top of the web browser that you're using.

URLs tell your browser exactly where to go to retrieve an individual Web page, and every URL is totally unique. A typical one looks something like this:

```
http://www.myfirmname.com
```

Just like a postal address, a URL, or Internet address, is made up of several sections. Postal addresses, of course, include the following information:

✔ Name of the recipient

✔ Street address of the recipient

✔ City, state, zip code, and sometimes country of the recipient

Internet addresses are also made up of standard parts. In the Internet address `http://www.myfirmname.com`, the different URL sections are:

✔ `http://`

✔ `www.`

✔ `myfirmname`

✔ `.com`

In the following sections, we take a look at each of these parts to see what it means and how it helps direct messages to the right recipients.

The key to http://

The first section of the URL example — `http://` — tells the computer what protocol (or language) it should use. The abbreviation HTTP actually stands for HyperText Transfer Protocol, the common language used by all computers on the World Wide Web. When a URL starts with `http://`, it is telling the computer that it is supposed to find and retrieve a specific Web page for viewing.

In some cases, URLs may start with other types of transfer protocols, which tell the computer to perform different kinds of operations. For example,

✔ `ftp://` informs the computer to use the File Transfer Protocol. This is the language computers use to download files over the Internet.

✔ `gopher://` instructs the computer to retrieve text-only information from the Web. This protocol was more commonly used before the World Wide Web's graphical interface came into general use.

✔ `telnet://` is a protocol that enables you to access another computer over the Internet from a remote location.

When the computer knows what language it should use, it needs to know where it should go to retrieve the information. And that is the function of the remaining sections of the URL.

The role of www.

After the // in a URL, you often see the three letters www. If you have already guessed that www stands for World Wide Web, you're right. Those three letters plus the domain name, which comes next, tell your computer exactly which set of Web pages it should retrieve at the IP address you've specified. Although www. is by far the most common domain name prefix, it is not the only one that people can use.

For example, suppose you have a company called Top Widgets, and you've set up a Web site with separate sets of Web pages for your retail customers, wholesale customers, and suppliers. To keep those sets of information separate, you've arranged with your Web hosting provider (a company that makes your Web address accessible over the Internet) to label the pages separately with the following URLs:

- ✔ http://www.topwidgets.com for retail customer Web pages
- ✔ http://shop.topwidgets.com for wholesale customer Web pages
- ✔ http://topwidgets.com for supplier pages

The domain name Topwidgets.com directs everyone — retailers, wholesalers, and suppliers — to the correct IP address for your Web site. The prefixes www. and shop. — or the lack of a prefix, in the last example — direct each group to its appropriate Web page.

If you want a prefix other than www., you can usually contact your Web hosting provider to arrange it.

The domain name: The power to choose

After the prefix www., in most cases, comes the domain name. This is the section of the URL that people most commonly select. Domain names can be made up of letters and numbers, alone or in combination. They can also contain hyphens, but never at the beginning or end of the domain name. For example, 4-movies.com is an acceptable domain name, but -4-movies.com is not. Spaces between characters are never allowed, and neither are special characters like @, _, #, $, !, %, *, or &.

Today, domain names may contain as many as 67 characters. That's far more than most people would probably find practical. Some argue, however, that it could make good marketing sense to turn a long, memorable phrase into an unforgettable domain name, like:

Abirdinthehandisworthtwointhebush.org

Memorable, yes — but probably also hard to spell correctly when you're in a hurry. We cover more about the pros and cons of domain name length in Chapter 4.

TLDs: Domain name suffixes

The last part of the URL in our example — .com — is a *TLD* or *top-level domain* (also known as an *extension*). TLDs are suffixes that indicate the type of individual or organization that possesses the Internet address. A number of different types of TLDs exist:

- ✔ **Generic top-level domains (gTLDs):** Available to anyone from any country who registers or purchases a domain name.
- ✔ **Restricted TLDs:** Only available to specific types of organizations.
- ✔ **Country-code top-level domains (ccTLDs):** Issued by individual nations according to their own rules and regulations.

In the following sections, we look closely at each type of TLD and the options that may be available to you when you acquire a domain name.

Generic TLDs: Open to Everyone

Generic TLDs (gTLDs) are the usual choices available to anyone around the world who wants a domain name for business, personal, or organizational use. There are three different gTLDs — .com, .net, and .org. In practice, all the gTLDs are functionally the same, but .com is by far the most valuable and popular extension.

In the following sections, we take a look at each of the gTLDs and see what it means in today's domain name marketplace.

The world's top choice: .com

By far the most common, recognizable, and sought-after TLD around the world is .com. Originally, .com was designed as an address category for commercial businesses. Today, however, the .com TLD can be used by anyone for any purpose. It has become so widespread that the term .com has come to stand for the whole phenomenon of Internet enterprise.

Many people believe that a .com suffix conveys more seriousness and credibility than other gTLDs. And that point of view is borne out by the marketplace. Fully 80 percent of all domain names use the .com TLD. And in the domain name resale market, .org and .net TLDs command only a fraction of the value of sought-after .com names (we go into domain name values in much more detail in Chapter 10).

The #2 choice: .net

Originally, .net was intended as a TLD for business and organizations involved in network administration and other Internet infrastructure activities. These days, though, .net — like the other gTLDs — may be used by any individual, business, or organization without restriction.

Although the .net TLD is second in popularity to .com, it does not come close to matching the .com phenomenon. The .net extension is used in only 12 percent of all domain name registrations.

In third place: .org

Most commonly, the .org TLD is used by nonprofit organizations, but it can also be used by anyone around the world who acquires a domain name. It is the least popular gTLD, however; only 8 percent of Internet addresses use the .org extension.

Off-Limits: Restricted-Access TLDs

In addition to the generic top-level domains (TLDs), there are some TLDs that are reserved for restricted uses:

- ✔ .edu: Issued only to degree-granting educational institutions in the United States.

- ✔ .gov: Issued by the General Services Administration and may be used only by organizations and agencies of the United States government.

- ✔ .mil: Issued by the United States Department of Defense and reserved exclusively for use by the U.S. military.

- ✔ .int: Restricted to organizations established by international treaties between governments, including some agencies and organizations of the United Nations.

Unlike gTLDs, restricted TLDs convey important information about the Internet address holders and their official positions or affiliations.

The Wide World of Country-Code TLDs

Beyond the gTLDs and restricted TLDs, there is a whole world of country-code TLDs (ccTLDs) linked to specific nations, many of which are available to all domain name registrants. The ccTLDs are based on the International Telecommunications Union codes for nations and territories worldwide. Nearly 250 countries have their own ccTLDs, for which they allow domain name registrations according to their individual regulations.

All ccTLDs are made up of two letters — for example, .uk is the ccTLD for the United Kingdom and .al is the ccTLD for Albania. About 90 country-code TLDs are unrestricted, which means that anyone can acquire one on a first-come, first-served basis. Other ccTLDs, however, have strict rules that may require, for example, a local presence or business operation in that nation. For example, France requires registrants for its .fr ccTLD to have offices in France and to incorporate their businesses there.

Many people are interested in having a ccTLD suffix for their domain name because of the global nature of the Internet. Even if you operate a local or regional business in the U.S., the Internet suddenly gives you access to potential customers around the world. By registering your domain name with different ccTLDs, especially in countries where you sell your services or products, you can minimize consumer confusion and protect your brand (we cover more on these issues in Part III).

Other people are interested in registering domain names with ccTLDs because it vastly expands the range of names they can select. Of the more than 24 million domain names that have been registered ending in .com, .net, and .org, more than half use the .com TLD. The popularity of the .com TLD has seriously limited the number of .com names that are available. But the same domain name that is no longer available as a .com — for example, Go.com — may be available with an unrestricted ccTLD such as Go.to or Go.md.

The tricky part is finding out what the different registration requirements are for the ccTLDs you want. You can find a complete list of ccTLDs in Appendix A. But if you're interested in registering your domain name with one of the ccTLDs, you can turn to the Internet Assigned Numbers Authority (IANA) Web site at www.iana.org/cctld/cctld-whois.htm for the contact information for each ccTLD.

In the meantime, here's a glimpse of some of the many ccTLD options.

Surfing South Pacific ccTLDs

Amazingly, one-tenth of all the world's ccTLDs belong to South Pacific nations, many of them little-known islands such as Nieue and Tuvalu. A number of these are available to all domain name registrants. Here are just a few.

What's .nu?

The .nu suffix is the unrestricted ccTLD for the South Pacific nation of Nieue, a 40-mile-wide coral island. The .nu suffix has achieved some popularity because it sounds like the word *new* in English, and it means "nude" in French and "now" in the Scandinavian tongues. It has already been used for domain names such as Its.nu and Really.nu. Go to nunames.nu for more information on the .nu ccTLD.

The .tv listing

Another Pacific nation, Tuvalu — a collection of coral islands 2,500 miles northeast of Australia — has been registering domain names in its .tv ccTLD. Not surprisingly, the suffix has been marketed mainly to television and entertainment-oriented companies. For details, you can go to www.tv.

Please .cc me

Until recently, few people had ever heard of the tiny Cocos Islands, an Australian territory in the eastern Indian Ocean with a population of only 650. Its .cc TLD, however, is now being actively marketed worldwide. You can learn more about it at www.nic.cc.

Tonga .to go

His Royal Highness Crown Prince Tupouto'a, of the Kingdom of Tonga in the Friendly Islands, has also opened his nation's ccTLD to the world, registering domain names from the country's consulate in San Francisco. The .to suffix — which has been an appealing alternative for some travel-related companies — is registered by Tonic Domains at tonic.to.

When you need an .md

The Republic of Moldova, formerly part of the Soviet Union, is a tiny country in the northern Balkans, located between Romania and Ukraine. Thanks to the Internet, Moldova has also become a hot spot for domain name registrations lately, and not just for Moldovans. The ccTLD for Moldova is .md, and it's unrestricted. Although those two letters have no particular meaning in Romanian and Russian — the two languages spoken in Moldova — they have a lot of meaning for physicians in the English-speaking countries around the world. For more information about Moldova's .md ccTLD, you can check out www.register.md.

America is .us

The official ccTLD for the United States is .us, and it's available to state and local governments as well as individuals, organizations, businesses, schools, libraries, and museums. The University of Southern California's Information Sciences Institute handles registrations for .us. You can go to www.nic.us for information.

On the Horizon: The New TLDs

To help relieve the shortage of .com, .org, and .net domain names, the Internet Corporation for Assigned Names and Numbers (ICANN) has agreed to create a slew of brand new TLDs. The suffixes are:

- ✔ .aero for the transport industry
- ✔ .biz for general use
- ✔ .coop for business cooperatives
- ✔ .info for general use
- ✔ .museum for museums
- ✔ .name for personal Internet addresses
- ✔ .pro for professionals, such as doctors and lawyers.

The big, unanswered question is whether these new TLDs will really increase the number and quality of available domain names — or whether branded companies such as Wine will simply snap up Wine.biz and Wine.info, resulting in continuing domain name shortages as well as increased trademark infringement issues.

Chapter 3

The New "Land Rush" in Domain Names

- -

In This Chapter

▶ Making sense of the booming market in domain name "real estate"

▶ Knowing why the domain name marketplace is heating up

▶ Getting to know some winners in the domain name game

- -

*I*n today's environment of dwindling supply and skyrocketing demand, the value of Internet domain name property is booming. In response, a huge new resale market has sprung up, enabling businesses and individuals to buy domain names from each other. In this chapter, we take a look at the new domain name real estate market and a few individuals who have turned their domain name assets into gold.

Understanding the Reasons Behind Skyrocketing Domain Name Prices

Like the most sought-after real estate, the demand for domain names has soared in the last few years. Back in 1995, only 100,000 domain names had been registered. But by the end of 2000, the number of registered names had soared to more than 24 million — and according to some estimates, 140 million domain names will be registered by 2003.

What's driving this booming market? For one thing, many people are only now realizing that they need a domain name to take part in the new Internet economy. As e-commerce takes off, having a domain name is becoming an essential asset for large and small businesses alike. By the end of 1999, more than 119 million Americans were actively surfing and shopping on the Internet — up from just 53 million worldwide the year before.

Unfortunately, many people are also finding out that most of the best domain names have already been claimed. Just about any word in English, as well as single words prefixed by the letters *i* or *e,* are gone — as are most combinations of two letters. In fact, according to a study by *Wired News,* of the 25,500 standard dictionary words, fewer than 1,760 are still available.

In many ways, the domain name market is similar to a land-rush phenomenon. Many of those who were lucky enough to register prime domain names when they were plentiful have been able to sell them at huge profits as the market took off. Between 1998 and 2000, top sales of domain names rocketed from $150,000 to an astonishing $7.5 million! Of course, most domain names tend to sell for considerably less, and average prices hover around $40,000. When you consider that most sellers acquired these domain names for $100 or $70, however, they are pretty significant investments.

The rise in domain name resale prices has surprised even those who have always been bullish on their values. Back in 1997, for example, one domain name dealer said he "wouldn't be surprised" if sales shot up as high as $750,000 or $1 million. But only a year later, in 1998, Compaq Computer Corporation paid $3.35 million to buy the name AltaVista.com for its AltaVista search engine. And by 1999, domain name sales were routinely soaring past the million-dollar mark. That year, Virtual Vineyards, an Internet wine seller, spent $3 million to acquire the domain name Wine.com. CarsDirect.com shelled out $2.2 million for the Autos.com address, an offshore gambling company successfully bid $1.03 million for the name Wallstreet.com, and a southern California company paid a record-setting $7.5 million for Business.com.

The domain name resale market is by far the hottest for .com, the most prestigious domain name suffix. If a domain name is a location in cyberspace, a .com name is the most prized business address, like New York's Fifth Avenue or L.A.'s Rodeo Drive. Of course, there are still plenty of available domain names — any name that uses up to 67 letters or numbers (including the TLD) can be registered — and there are lots of .org and .net names to choose from, along with plenty of ccTLDs. But the fact of the matter is that in most cases, the short, memorable, desirable names, especially the sought-after .com names, are running out. Savvy Internet investors saw this coming early, and some have profited beyond their wildest dreams. We take a look at a few of these in the following sections.

Business.com: An Investor's Dream

One of the savvy investors who profited from a great domain name is Houston-based entrepreneur Marc Ostrofsky. Back in 1992, Ostrofsky, the owner of a publishing and trade show company, guessed that domain names might one day be the 800-numbers of the future. "My hunch was that a good, memorable domain name could someday have the same identity and branding power of a telemarketing idea like 1-800-FLOWERS," he said.

Two years later, Ostrofsky acted on his intuition. He registered 80 domain names for a total investment of $8,000 — snapping up a collection of generic names such as Ebusiness.com, Eflowers.com, Eradio.com, and Etickets.com. "I figured that I could invest that $8,000 or leave it in a bank earning 5 percent interest," he said. "It was a leap of faith, but I believed that one day those names might be worth a lot."

Then, in 1996, Ostrofsky decided to make a much bigger bet. As part of his company's publishing plan, he wanted to launch a new magazine called *Business.com,* but he found out that a London-based computer company, Business Systems International (BSI), owned that particular domain name. So Ostrofsky made BSI an offer to purchase the name. After an escalating, two-month bidding war, Ostrofsky successfully bought the Business.com name for what was then the world's-record price of $150,000. The event made world-wide headlines, because no one had ever spent that kind of money to purchase a domain name, an invisible piece of Internet real estate.

The British owners thought they'd made a killing — $150,000 in pure profit for a domain name they had registered for free. And many observers believed Ostrofsky had made a big mistake. "People thought I was out of my mind," Ostrofsky said. But even then, he was confident that he'd made the better deal. "It takes money to make money," he said, "and in this business, it also take timing. You have to be patient, and you have to understand the value of what you have."

Three years later, Ostrofsky's timing — and investments — paid off. In February 1999, he made his first domain name sale, turning over the Eflowers.com name to an online florist, Flowers Direct, for $25,000 in cash. As part of the sale, Ostrofsky also negotiated 50 cents for each transaction on the site and a bouquet of flowers delivered to anyone he chooses, each month for the rest of his life.

But that was just the beginning of Ostrofsky's winning streak. At the end of the year, two companies began contacting him with serious offers to purchase the domain name Business.com. At first, Ostrofsky wasn't interested. He had recently sold his publishing and trade show company for a healthy sum, and he intended to keep the Business.com domain name for his own use. But when the bidding went well over $5 million, Ostrofsky thought it was time to make a deal. In December 1999, he turned around and sold the Business.com name for the stunning sum of $7.5 million, a figure that dwarfed all previous domain name sales.

According to Jake Winebaum — whose company paid the record-setting sale price to Ostrofsky — the domain name Business.com is "a prime piece of real estate" that's worth every cent of its $7.5 million price tag. Winebaum — founder of eCompanies, a firm that "incubates" Internet startups — plans to use it for developing new Internet business-to-business services.

The Business.com name was considered so valuable because it's clear, simple, straightforward, and easy to understand and remember. In the increasingly crowded Internet marketplace, those qualities mean that ecompanies may be able to save millions on advertising and marketing — money it would otherwise have to spend to "brand" its domain name in the minds of potential customers. Simplicity counts these days, because building brands with obscure domain names such as Amazon or Yahoo! is a lot more expensive than it once was. With a premium name like Business.com, Winebaum declared, "our marketing dollars will go much farther because we won't have to explain what it is."

"You've got to know when to hold them and when to fold them," Ostrofsky says. And today, he is still holding onto acres of potentially lucrative domain name property. His portfolio now includes more than 100 domain names, most of which he registered for $70 to $100 each. With time and patience, he believes, many of those names, too, could skyrocket in value. "Right now," he explained, "some names are selling for $20,000 to $80,000 that could potentially be worth millions. The market for domain names is still very undervalued, even for marquis names that are worth a high premium."

For now, the sale of Business.com has not changed Ostrofsky's quality of life — but it *has* altered the way people look at him and his once-unconventional investments in domain names. "The sale of Business.com amazed people," he said. "Now, everybody thinks that I know something that they don't. Usually," he added, "I'm the guy who says, 'Hell, why didn't I think of that?' — but I guess it's my turn to be a step ahead."

Loans.com: Patience Pays off

Friends of Marcelo Siero were stunned in January 2000, when the northern California engineer auctioned off his domain name Loans.com to financial giant Bank of America for $3 million. "They couldn't believe it," said Siero, who resides in the small, coastal mountain town of Ben Lomond, two hours south of San Francisco.

But Siero himself wasn't a bit surprised by the sale price. Back in 1994, when he originally registered the domain name for free — along with five other names including Houses.com, Romance.com, Artists.com, and Lawoffices.com — he was confident that he'd made a profitable move. At the time, Siero ran a small business as an Internet Service Provider (ISP), and he planned to use the domain names to provide e-mail services for his small commercial customers. Pretty soon, though, Siero realized that the most valuable part of his business was the portfolio of domain names he'd acquired. Even then, he remembers, "I thought that someday several of them would be worth over $1 million apiece."

For years, though, the market lagged behind Siero's expectations. Even in 1998, he said, "I don't think I could have gotten more than $100,000 for the domain name Loans.com." In fact, that year, Siero offered to sell three of his most valuable domain names — Loans.com, Houses.com, and Romance.com — to a potential buyer for a package price of $600,000 in order to raise money for another business opportunity. "Fortunately for me," he said, "the guy I offered the deal to turned me down."

By January 1999, however, domain name values were going through the roof, and Siero decided that the time was right to sell. He put Loans.com up for auction with a reserve price of $3 million; if no bidder stepped up to that price, he planned to take the domain name off the market. But this time, the marketplace confirmed Siero's hopes. After a brief bidding war, Bank of America offered $3 million, cash, for Loans.com, and the deal was closed.

Even though he's happy with the price, Siero is certain the bidding would have gone much higher if the banking industry had been more tuned into the business value of domain names and the Internet. "If you think of the Internet as a MONOPOLY board, Loans.com is Broadway for the lending industry," he explained. "It's the natural domain name — the easiest to remember and type in. But most banks, like many traditional businesses, don't have that vision yet. If they had," he added, "the bidding could have really gone sky-high."

Siero, meanwhile, is developing some of his other domain names into Internet-based businesses. He is building Houses.com into a commission-free online real estate portal, and Artists.com will be a site for up-and-coming artists on the Web.

Drugs.com: Rx for Profit

Success has come even to those, like Eric MacIver, who only recently entered the domain name market. In May 1999, the 20-year-old Mesa, Arizona, Web designer took out a purchase option on the domain name Drugs.com. Just three and a half months later, he sold the name at auction — and though Drugs.com didn't quite fetch a million dollars, it came close. On MacIver's 21st birthday — a coming-of-age experience he's not likely to forget — he closed the domain name sale for more than $823,000, or about $103,000 per letter.

Entrepreneurship comes naturally to MacIver, who was peddling rocks door-to-door to neighbors when he was only 3 years old. In 1998, at age 19, he dropped out of Northern Arizona University to start his own Web design and development company, Sandline Productions, funding it with his $3,000 in savings. That year, MacIver also bought his first domain name, Websites.com, from its original registrant in order to promote his business. The experience quickly taught him the marketing value of a choice, generic name. The Websites.com domain name brought Sandline 250 potential customers a day, people who had simply typed *websites* into their browser bar. Some 50 percent of Sandline's clients, MacIver said, contacted his business that way.

The next year, MacIver was thinking about launching an online pharmacy or bath and beauty business. As a first step, he contacted Bonnie Neubeck, a Web marketing professional in Minneapolis who had registered the domain name Drugs.com in 1994. In May, Neubeck agreed to let MacIver have a purchase option on the name, and two months later — after he had dropped his online pharmacy idea — he and Neubeck agreed to put the Drugs.com domain name up for auction. Their asking price was $260,000.

Although bidding stuck at around $110,000 for a week, offers started climbing fast on the last day — rising from $555,555 at 5:00 p.m. to $750,123 at 5:15 p.m., and finally to $823,456 at 5:25 p.m., the auction's close. It was an exciting moment for MacIver, who was fielding phone calls from *Good Morning America,* and it was equally gratifying for Neubeck. Earlier that year, she had tried — unsuccessfully — to sell the name Drugs.com directly to pharmaceutical companies. "I was sure drug companies would jump at this domain name right away," she said, "but, amazingly, they didn't realize what a great investment it would be."

The winning bidder, however, clearly understood the name's potential. The buyer — a San Francisco Internet investment company called Venture Frogs — planned to use the domain name for a new drug and pharmacy portal on the Net. Even at a price of more than $800,000, the Venture Frogs team felt they got a bargain, given the $102 billion U.S. market for prescription drugs. "In terms of branding on the Internet," explained company cofounder Tony Hsieh, having a great domain name "means a lot right now. If it's not unusual for someone to spend $10 million to $20 million on marketing to improve their brand, it certainly wouldn't be unreasonable for them to pay a fraction of that, say 10 percent, to buy a domain name. It's a bit too early to go into any specifics, but," he noted, "Drugs.com has the potential to be worth much, much more than we paid for it."

With the Drugs.com sale under her belt, Neubeck is considering putting several of her other domain names — Infocenter.com, Netprofit.com, and Internetbroadcastingcorporation.com — on the market. As for MacIver, he's invested most of his Drugs.com earnings in his business, a software company called Meshware (at `meshware.com`).

Skateboards.com: Betting on the Future

The next generation of domain name millionaires *may* well include young visionaries such as 15-year-old Camden DeLong, the son of California physician and Internet investor Kent DeLong.

In 1997, as a blond, fresh-faced eighth-grader, Camden persuaded his father to register the domain name Exboards.com so he could use it for a small retail Web site he created, selling skateboards and snowboards to his friends at school. The next year, inspired by Camden's entrepreneurial spirit, his father purchased the domain name Skateboards.com for $125,000, along with the phone number 1-800-SKATEBOARD. Camden immediately went to work to develop the name's marketing potential.

"Skateboards.com has instant name recognition, and I realized it could be an instant brand," Camden explained. So at age 15, he got into the skateboard manufacturing business, ordering a line of boards made to his own personal specifications — branded with the Skateboards.com name and a logo he designed.

"I can make a better profit margin by retailing my own Skateboards.com line," Camden said. "The manufacturer ships me the custom boards, then I package them and send them out myself." Camden is even building the Skateboards.com brand by sponsoring skaters and launching a new Web site designed by another 15-year-old Internet entrepreneur.

"My friends think Skateboards.com is cool," Camden acknowledges. But that's not what drives his interest in the business. He has bigger plans. "I've always wanted to be the CEO of a major company," he said, and Skateboards.com, he thinks, could eventually turn into one. Just in case, though, he and his dad have put the Skateboards.com domain name up for auction. For now, at least, Camden is not inclined to sell — at least for anything less than a million-dollar offer. "I know that this is what I'm going to do for the rest of my life," he said. "If I sell out too early, I know I'd be giving up too much."

Part II
Finding the Right Domain Name

The 5th Wave

By Rich Tennant

"Hey—here's a company that develops short memorable domain names for new businesses. It's listed at www.CompanyThatDevelopsShort-MemorableDomainNamesForNewBusinesses.com."

In this part . . .

Buying a domain name is about a whole lot more than just randomly picking a word and attaching a .com to it. So in the chapters in this part, we give you some great tips for actually choosing a name that will accomplish what you want it to — whether that's drawing customers to your business or steering friends and family to your personal Web site. We also let you know how to go about actually registering that name after you've arrived on it — complete with details for what to do if (gasp!) the name you want is already taken.

Chapter 4

Choosing a Domain Name and Extension

. . . .

In This Chapter

▶ Knowing what's in a name

▶ Finding the best possible name

▶ Getting creative help with the naming process

▶ Picking the right extension

. . . .

*W*hether you want a business, organizational, or personal presence on the Net, selecting a domain name is the most important place to start. Your domain name should communicate the message or image you *want* to communicate. It should make it easy for people to reach you on the Web, and it should at least hint at the value that you offer.

Unfortunately, selecting a great name has gotten harder, thanks to the sheer volume of domain names that have already been registered. Until 1993, only 200 to 300 domain names were registered each month; today, more than 270,500 domain names are registered every *week,* according to the Internet Corporation for Assigned Names and Numbers (ICANN).

But take heart. There are still plenty of great names out there; you just need some creativity and patience to find them. In this chapter, we explore what you can do to select the best possible domain names.

Thinking about What You Want Your Domain Name to Convey

A domain name is your identity on the Web. It communicates many messages not only about the nature of what you have to offer but also the perceived value of your business. Clearly, putting your best foot forward with a name that works positively for you makes sense. For example, a domain name like Ripoff.com obviously gets across a message, but it's probably not one that will work to your advantage.

Most people want a domain name to communicate one or more of the following messages:

- ✔ **The name of your company's business.** If you have an existing business, this is the best possible idea, because anyone who knows your company name will know how to find you on the Net. Many of your existing customers, in fact, will probably try to find your Web site by typing in your business name, followed by a .com. You will save them a lot of frustration and confusion if that is actually the domain name that you use.

  Not all company names make good domain names, especially if they are very long or hard to spell. MBNA Corporation, for example, started out with the lengthy domain name Mbnainternational.com, but then switched to the much-shorter name Mbna.com. Sensibly, the retailer Hammacher Schlemmer went ahead and registered the domain name Hammacherschlemmer.com, but uses the much shorter (and easier to spell) Hammacher.com for its e-commerce site.

- ✔ **What you offer.** A domain name can't ensure business success, but a good domain name can enhance your odds of establishing an effective presence on the Net. Most businesses benefit from a descriptive name that gets their product and service offerings across. Although some of the most famous domain names, like Amazon.com and Yahoo.com, are not the least bit descriptive, they have had the benefit of huge amounts of press and advertising spending to help explain to consumers what they do. Today, because the Internet has become increasingly crowded with sites clamoring for attention, companies need to explain their offerings with their domain names or spend a lot of extra money trying to get that basic information across.

  For that mythical manufacturer, the widget maker, for example, a domain name like Topwidgets.com or 123widgets.com is much better than a pleasant but nondescriptive name like Skybluehorizon.com.

Many people also want their domain name to:

- ✔ **Get people's attention.** Sometimes, a domain name can work best by being distinctive rather than literally explaining a site's offerings. In 1999, for example, an information technology services company with a straightforward name, Computerliteracy.com, switched its domain name to the relatively daring Fatbrain.com and drew a lot more Internet traffic as a result.

- ✔ **Create a brand.** In the physical world, you establish a brand identity through your product advertising, packaging, and marketing. On the Internet, however, your main branding opportunity is your domain name — a much less costly item. If you have a domain name that uses your product's name — such as Skateboards.com — you reinforce the brand and make it easy for customers to find your product on the Net.

✔ **Reflect their identity.** You can do this, for example, by turning personal elements such as nicknames, street names, or family names into interesting and unusual Internet monikers.

Coming Up with a Good Domain Name

Despite the fact that so many words and combinations have already been taken, there are still millions of possible domain names available. Especially now that domain names can have up to 67 characters (including the TLD), the supply is practically infinite.

You can also use numerals and hyphens in a domain name to distinguish them from names that have already been registered. For example, the domain name Formovies.com may no longer be available, but 4-movies.com could be a viable substitute.

Be careful when using dashes and numerals in your domain name. As many dot-com companies learned when they launched radio advertising campaigns, you need extra time, money, and effort to communicate the spelling of domain names that include those elements.

How should you get started? Depending on your situation, you may want to brainstorm domain name ideas on your own or assemble a team of friends, coworkers or employees to give you a hand.

If you put a brainstorming team together, make sure that it is not too big to be effective or too small to include important points of view.

Coming up with a great domain name is not rocket science, and in many cases it does not require professional help. Keep in mind that the folks who started Yahoo! came up with the name themselves. Whether you want to think up a great name on your own or with a group, the following sections give you some advice for making your brainstorming as productive as possible.

Make a master idea list

Start off by writing down anything and everything that comes to mind, no matter how crazy it may seem. Try to accumulate as many possible names as you or your team can think of. At this stage of the game, don't try to edit or second-guess the ideas. What you want is a master list of every conceivable variation, flash of brilliance, and seemingly silly suggestion. This is the master list that you'll edit down later (and maybe come back to again for more ideas).

To make your master list as exhaustive as possible, use a thesaurus and dictionary so that you can jot down synonyms and related words. There are even online thesauri that you can use at `www.thesaurus.com` and at `www.m-w.com/thesaurus.htm`.

Here are some tips for putting your master domain name list together. Think about:

- ✔ **Analogies of words that you like.** For example, if you like the word *super* in your domain name, consider alternatives like *best, top, wonder,* and so on.

- ✔ **Combinations of words.** Combining two or more words in a domain name is an especially good strategy because almost all the single words in the English language have been registered.

- ✔ **Fanciful words.** Many companies have developed successful brand names based on creative words like Coca-Cola, and Kodak. Your imagination is your only limitation.

Keep in mind that a fanciful word generally does not describe the product or service, so you may need to heavily support your domain name with advertising.

- ✔ **Domain names used by your competitors.** The name you select should set you apart and above the competition. If your competitor is using the straightforward domain name 123widgets.com, for instance, you could get across a more positive marketing message — and enhance your company's perceived value — with a descriptive domain name like Topwidgets.com or Wonderwidgets.com.

Speaking the global language of the Internet

Remember that the Internet is a global marketplace, and be sure to check the meaning of your domain name in other languages. The ten languages that are spoken most commonly around the world are:

- ✔ Chinese, Mandarin
- ✔ Spanish
- ✔ English
- ✔ Bengali
- ✔ Hindi
- ✔ Portuguese
- ✔ Russian
- ✔ Japanese
- ✔ German
- ✔ Chinese, Wu

Narrow down your list

After you have created your master list, look it over and make note of your favorite ideas on a second, short list of possible domain names. When you're considering candidates for this list, keep these domain name tips in mind:

- ✔ **Make it short.** Many people maintain that a domain name with 7 characters or less — like a telephone number — is an ideal length that is easy for people to remember, but 10 or 12 characters can work fine, too. Remember that the shorter the domain name is, the simpler it is to remember and the quicker it is to type. Plus, if you plan to advertise your domain name at some point, a shorter name has many benefits. Short names are often easier for radio announcers to pronounce, and they are quicker for people to read on billboards as they drive by.

- ✔ **Keep it simple.** Complex or obscure domain names — like 2hrspxyc-inc.com — may be extremely hard for people to remember. Also, try to avoid an acronym, unless the acronym is better recognized by people than the words it stands for. Generally speaking, registering your company's full name, even if it is long, is better than registering an acronym that no one will recognize. The best option is to register your firm's full name as well as the acronym, if they are both available — that way, customers will be able to reach you through both addresses.

- ✔ **Make it memorable.** A domain name that is top of mind, like About.com, Liquidaudio.com, or Cars.com will likely bring your Web site much more traffic than a name that's more obscure, because people won't be scratching their heads trying to remember your domain name. A good way to come up with a memorable name is to see what words pop into your own mind first when you think of your products or services that you plan to offer on the Net. Use those top-of-mind words when you make your master and secondary lists.

- ✔ **Make it easy to say and spell.** There's a guideline for almost every commercial name: Make sure that people can pronounce it. Word of mouth won't do much good for a company with a domain name like Zzyphthix.com. Couple that with a second guideline for domain names: Make sure that people can spell it. If a domain name is difficult to spell, your site will be considerably more difficult to find.

- ✔ **Make it evocative.** What emotional responses does the name inspire? If it's a positive emotion, it could give your Web brand personality and help inspire customer loyalty.

- ✔ **Avoid negative or offensive meanings.** This applies in English as well as in other languages, because the Internet is a global environment. This point is an especially important one to remember if you'll be marketing your products or services overseas. Always check the meaning of domain names with native foreign language speakers to make sure that they are not offensive to non-English-speaking audiences.

✔ **Say it out loud.** Seeing how the name sounds when it is spoken is especially important if you may be considering radio or TV advertising in the future, or if your domain name could be developed into a brand name. If you have to go out of your way to explain numbers, hyphens, or spelling, then it's probably not the best possible domain name.

✔ **Try adding an *e* or an *i* as a prefix.** These prefixes have come to denote Internet-based businesses. Many single words with these prefixes have already been registered, but you can try them in combination with two or more short words, like Emagnetsusa.com.

Test out the names

If you're going to be using your domain name for business, testing out your short list on current and potential customers, coworkers, and friends is a good idea. After all, choosing a business domain name is a major move. You don't want to pick a name that will end up confusing customers or driving them away. And because you've spent so much time thinking about the domain names on your list, you may not be as objective as outsiders in figuring out whether the name works.

Getting Help from Computer Naming Programs

If you keep staring at blank sheets of paper and hitting the wall when you try to come up with a list of possible domain names, one solution is to turn to your computer for help. A number of online naming programs and software packages are available, and you may find that these are useful tools. Free online naming programs on the Web include:

✔ Name Boy (`www.nameboy.com`)

✔ Domain Fellow (`www.domainfellow.com`)

✔ 123Finder (`www.123finder.com`)

In addition, free, low-cost and higher-end programs on the market include:

✔ **Domain Name Analyzer,** a freeware program for Windows, available at `www.findgoodnames.com`.

✔ **NamePro,** available for $495 at `www.namestormers.com`.

✔ **NameWave,** also from Namestormers at `www.namestormers.com`, can generate up to 200 possible names, all for just $15.

✔ **IdeaFisher,** available for $697 at `www.ideacenter.com`.

Getting Help from a Professional Naming Agency

If you have a larger budget and would like to hire professional help, numerous professional naming agencies can assist you. Generally speaking, agency fees can range from $2,000 to $20,000 or more for domain name generation services.

Although each agency uses its own professional naming methodology, many rely on these basic steps to come up with a name that works for you:

1. **Meet to discuss your naming goals.**

   At this initial stage, the agency will talk with you about important factors such as your products or services, marketing focus, competition, the image and tone you want to convey, what your company is today, and what its plans are for the future.

2. **Review any background information you provide.**

   The agency will look at all the information they gather in Step 1 along with other materials such as reports, brochures, ads, and business plans.

3. **Present an initial list of possible names.**

   Like the master list we discuss earlier in this chapter, the agency's pre-liminary list is wide-ranging and can include anywhere from several dozen to more than a thousand names.

4. **Present a second, refined list.**

   After a screening process, the agency will winnow the initial list down to a much shorter, focused list of possible alternatives.

5. **Check to see if the domain names are available and whether they are clear of trademark issues.**

   As an important final step, many agencies will check the names on this short list to make sure that they are available and do not infringe on any existing trademarks. (We cover more on this part of the process in Chapter 5 and in all of Part III.)

A few of the many agencies that provide domain name services are:

- **ABC Namebank** (www.abc.namebank.com)
- **NameBase** (www.namebase.com)
- **Name-It** (www.nameit.com)
- **Namestormers** (www.namestormers.com)
- **NameTrade** (www.nametrade.com)

Knowing Which Extensions to Consider

After you have a short list of domain names, you need to give some thought to which of the many extensions (or TLDs, short for *top-level domains*) you should consider. Although .com is by far the most common and popular TLD, many businesses register their domain names in all three generic TLDs (gTLDs) — .com, .org, and .net — to avoid customer confusion and protect their domain name from potential trademark infringement. Other options are the country-code TLDs (ccTLDs), a choice that is particularly appealing if you do business in another country. Which option is right for you? Read on to find out.

Getting a .com

Most people who acquire a domain name opt for a .com. Today, the .com TLD is internationally recognized as shorthand for online business. This symbolic significance leads many people to demand it despite the relative shortage of desirable .com names. Another advantage of .com is that many browsers automatically insert that TLD after a domain name if no TLD has been specified. Even many overseas businesses, especially those that operate globally, prefer the image and impact of a U.S.-associated .com to their own nation's ccTLDs.

The dominance of .coms was dramatically drilled home by the e-commerce advertising binge during the 1999 Super Bowl game. Internet businesses took to the TV airwaves at record-setting prices, including e-companies such as Hotjobs.com, Britannica.com. Monster.com., and Pets.com. What every single one of them promoted, in addition to their products, was the ever-present .com at the end of their company names.

Beyond .com

The price you pay for the .com TLD, however, is the shortage of available, quality names. If having a .com is not important to you, then .org and .net deserve a closer look. The differences that once existed among .com, .org, and .net have blurred over time, although .org still tends to imply that its user is a nonprofit organization. Network Solutions used to screen domain name applications to make sure that each registrant fit into the appropriate gTLD category, but it stopped that practice in 1995 as the domain name market exploded. Today, the .net and .org gTLDS offer wider selection — though with considerably less marketing cachet — than the .com standard.

What about the ccTLDs?

Think seriously about registering your domain name with a ccTLD if you operate your business internationally. If you market products or services in Great Britain, for example, a .co.uk extension (the version of the .uk ccTLD that is used for commercial enterprises) may make good business sense for you. But even if your market is national or local, you may want to consider one of the specialty ccTLDs that anyone can register, such as .md, .cc, .tv, .ws, or .to. Many domain names are available in these categories, and their distinctiveness can help set you apart in the increasingly crowded Internet environment.

Chapter 5

Registering Your Domain Name

In This Chapter

▶ Figuring out where to go to register a domain name

▶ Finding out if the domain name you want is available

▶ Comparing costs and features

▶ Registering a domain name, from start to finish

*A*fter you have come up with a list of names that you like, the next step is to find out if at any of those domain names are available. If at least one of them is free, you should probably plan to register it right away — or someone else may register it first. With thousands of domain names registered each day, the only thing you can count on is that good names do not have a long shelf life.

Your first task — checking on the availability of a domain name — is surprisingly easy. The hard part is being patient if, as frequently happens, the names you check have already been registered to someone else. When you do find a name that is available, registering it is a simple process.

In this chapter, we guide you step-by-step through the process of checking on a domain name's availability and registering it. We also fill you in on the costs and special features of domain name registrars.

Knowing Who Registers Domain Names

Until 1999, only one company, Network Solutions, provided domain name registration services to the public. Since then, however, the registration business has been opened up to competition, and today you can choose from at least 80 registrars worldwide.

In the United States alone, more than 30 accredited domain name registrars are in operation, providing a variety of services. In general, registrars fall into four main groups, which I cover in the following sections.

Multiservice registrars

Multiservice registrars, as the name indicates, provide a wide range of value-added services in addition to domain name registration — everything from e-mail forwarding to international registrations, from Web site-building tools to ebusiness support. Registrars in this one-stop-shopping category include:

- Catalog.com, Inc. (www.catalog.com)
- Namesecure.com, Inc. (www.namesecure.com)
- Network Solutions, Inc. (www.networksolutions.com)
- register.com (www.register.com)

Discount registrars

Discount registrars come with no frills and generally compete on cost, offering reduced prices for domain name registrations. Be aware, however, that some discount registrars may provide a less secure environment for registering and transferring domain names. Some discount registrars include:

- Domain Registration Services (www.dotearth.com)
- EnetRegistry.com Corporation (www.enetregistry.com)
- e-names.org (www.e-names.org)
- eNom, Inc. (www.enom.com)
- FirstDomain.net Domain Name Registration (www.firstdomain.net)
- GKG.NET, INC. (www.gkg.net)
- Registrars.com (www.registrars.com)
- Names4ever.com (names4ever.com)
- Parava Networks (www.naame.com)
- Stargate Communications, Inc. (www.stargateinc.com)

International registration specialists

International registration specialists provide the specialized service of registering domain names for a variety of worldwide country-code TLDs (ccTLDs). Some will also let you register your domain name in foreign character sets, such as Chinese, Japanese, and Korean. A small sampling of international providers include:

- Alldomains.com, Inc. (`www.alldomains.com`)
- DomainRegistry.com, Inc. (`www.domainregistry.com`)
- EasySpace Ltd. (`www.easyspace.com`)
- register.com (`www.register.com`)
- Network Solutions, Inc. (`www.networksolutions.com`)
- Speednames, Inc. (`www.speednames.com`)

Volume registration specialists

Volume registration specialists focus on the discount registration of multiple names, priced according to the number of domain names being registered. Like some discount registrars, some bulk registration specialists may provide a less secure registration and transfer environment. Registrars in the volume category include:

- BulkRegister.com (`www.bulkregister.com`)
- DomainDiscover (`www.domaindiscover.com`)
- DomainZoo.com, Inc. (`www.domainzoo.com`)
- DotRegistrar.com (`www.dotregistrar.com`)
- Dotster, Inc. (`www.dotster.com`)
- ItsYourDomain.com (`www.itsyourdomain.com`)
- Signature Domains, Inc. (`www.signaturedomains.com`)
- The N@meIT Corporation (`nameit.net`)
- The Registry at Info Avenue (`www.iaregistry.com`)

Looking At Registration Pricing and Plans

In the new competitive registration market, many companies offer a wide variety of pricing packages for basic registration of `.com`, `.net`, and `.org` domain names. Pricing is usually based on the length of time for which you buy rights to the name (at the end of the term, you will need to pay a renewal fee if you wish to maintain your domain name "lease"). Table 5-1 lists registration costs for individual names (costs vary from one registrar to the next)

Table 5-1	Basic Domain Name Registration Fees
Time Period	**Price Range**
1 year	$15–$35
2 years	$30–$70
3 years	$88–$105
5 years	$75–$175
10 years	$150–$350

In addition, many registrars specialize in volume, or *bulk,* registration of numerous domain names at once. This alternative makes sense for companies that need many domain names for their various product and service lines as well as for domain name investors who wish to register a large number of domain names at one time. Table 5-2 lists price ranges for bulk domain name registration (again, costs vary from one registrar to the next).

Table 5-2	Volume Domain Name Registration Fees
Number of Names	**Price Range**
1–99 domain names	$10–$15 per name
100–999 domain names	$8–$13 per name
1,000 or more domain names	$7–$11 per name

Prices for registering international ccTLD domain names also vary widely, depending on specific national registration policies and the prices offered by affiliated registrars. Table 5-3 provides a sampling of costs for some ccTLD registrations.

Table 5-3	Sample ccTLD Registration Fees	
ccTLD	**Time Period**	**Fee**
.fm (Micronesia)	2 years	$200
.il (Israel)	2 years	$70
.ky (Cayman Islands)	1 year	$199
.md (Moldova)	1 year	$299

ccTLD	Time Period	Fee
.ms (Montserrat)	1 year	$50
.sh (St. Helena)	1 year	$97
.to (Tonga)	2 years	$100
.uk (United Kingdom)	2 years	$79

Check out a number of registrars to compare their services and costs. As the number of accredited registrars grows and the market becomes even more competitive, you can expect to find an increasing variety of features and pricing plans.

Registering a Domain Name

The first step in registering a domain name is finding out whether the domain name you want is available. Domain name registrars make it easy to do this. In most cases, it takes only a matter of seconds to determine whether a specific name is available. But because so many names have already been snapped up, you may find yourself typing in dozens of names and variations before you find one that is available for use.

When you check on the availability of domain names, allow yourself plenty of time. That way, you'll have a better chance of coming up with successful alternatives to names that have already been taken. If you try to rush through the process, you may end up frustrated, out of time, and out of luck — without a domain name that you can use.

When you start checking on domain name availability, be sure to have your credit card information handy. That way, when you do find an available domain name that you like, you can register it immediately — before somebody else snaps it up instead.

To help you check on domain name availability, domain name registrars use a simple interface called *whois,* which compares a specific domain name you type in against the master record of names that have already been registered (a list currently maintained by Verisign Global Registry).

No matter which registrar you use, the whois interface works very much the same way. Usually, the whois tool appears as a blank search bar, preceded by www. on a registrar's home page. Figure 5-1 shows the whois search tool on the Network Solutions Web site.

Figure 5-1: Use the whois search tool at the Web site of any domain name registrar to check on availability of the domain name you're interested in.

Using whois to check a name is very simple. For example, if you want to see if the domain name Widgetworld.com is available, simply type "widgetworld" into the search bar and click Go.

Another screen appears with the results of your query. In this case, whois tells you that the domain name Widgetworld.com has already been taken. But helpfully, this registrar suggests alternatives to consider — domain names such as Mywidgetworld.com, E-widgetworld.com, and Widgetworldonline.com.

If your first-choice domain name is already taken and none of the alternatives presented by whois sound appealing, go back to your own short list of names and try again (and again and again, if necessary).

When you've found a domain name that you like — and that is available — you're ready to stake your claim. Registrars usually make the domain name registration process quick and easy. After you figure out that the domain name you want is available, you can follow the registrar's onscreen instructions to register the name for yourself.

When you register your domain name, you have to choose two *domain name servers,* which are special computers that make your domain name accessible on the Internet. Most registrars give you the option of having *them* take care of specifying a Web host for you. Or you can choose to specify your own domain name servers. Letting the registrar choose the Web hosts is the simplest approach, but if you choose your own Web hosts, you might be able to save a few bucks.

After you've registered a domain name, it should be available for use on the Internet within 72 hours (ccTLDs sometimes take several days to process).

Knowing What to Do After You've Registered

After you've registered a domain name, you can reserve it until you are ready to use it, develop it into a Web site, or use it for sending and receiving e-mail. Some registrars offer a wide range of services to help you take these next steps (in most cases, registrars charge additional fees for these extra services). In the following sections, we explain just a sampling of some of these features.

Domain name parking

If you don't want to use your domain name right away, many registrars will *park* (reserve) it for you until you are ready to put it into use for a Web site or e-mail. Some registrars will give you parking privileges for free.

If you know you won't be using your domain name right away, check around and find out which registrars allow free parking privileges before you register.

Web site design

Some multiservice registrars, including Network Solutions and register.com, offer a variety of services to help you design, publish, maintain, and update your Web site. Whether you're a Web site guru or you've never had your own site before, you can take advantage of these services to help you create the kind of Web site you're looking for.

E-mail forwarding

The e-mail forwarding feature enables you to use your domain name as a new e-mail address. Some registrars will help you set up a brand-new e-mail account that uses your domain name — for example, myname@myfirmname.com. If, on the other hand, you want to continue using your preexisting e-mail account —

for example, at the e-mail address myname@myinternetserviceprovider. com — many registrars will link it to your new domain name. That way, when people send you e-mail at your new domain name address, it will automatically be forwarded to the e-mail account you already use. In effect, your new domain name will be an alias for your existing e-mail address.

URL forwarding

Many registrars provide a service that links your new domain name to your preexisting Web site, so that traffic to your new address will be automatically forwarded to that URL. You can even choose to have numerous domain names linked to the same Web site. So, for example, if your company has changed names, you can make sure that people who know you by your new name and those who know you by your old name will all end up in the same place, no matter which domain name they use.

Part III
Navigating the Sometimes Rough Waters of Trademark Issues

The 5th Wave   By Rich Tennant

"I'm sorry Mr. Garret, a 35 year old tattoo doesn't qualify as a legal trademark for 'Mother.com'."

In this part . . .

Choosing a domain name is the fun part, but you need to be sure to pay attention to the details — and a big part of the details in the world of domain names is trademark issues. In this part, we let you know what specific issues pertain to domain names, so you can avoid problems before they start. We also let you know how to trademark your domain name so you can safeguard its use. Although the topic isn't exactly as much fun as surfing the Web, we get you in and out in no time (giving you the critical information you need), so you can move on to more enjoyable things.

Chapter 6

Understanding Trademarks

· ·

· ·

*A*nyone who registers a domain name should consider the trademark aspects before using it in a commercial manner. In most cases, the rights of trademark holders are stronger than the rights of domain name registrants. Although this is still a fast-changing area of the law, collisions between domain holders and trademark owners are likely to increase, especially because — like the number of domain names — the number of federally registered trademarks is skyrocketing.

The best thing you can do to protect yourself is to understand potential trademark problems and make sure that your domain name is free and clear of them before you register it or at least before you use it in your business. After all, when you set up a Web site and begin doing business on the Net, you will be making a big investment of your time and money — on everything from Web site design to promotional materials and business stationery. If, later on, you lose your domain name in a trademark conflict, the cost to your business can be significant, from the expense of printing new materials using your new domain name to the potential loss of customers who did business with you under your previous Internet address and won't remember to make the changeover.

In this chapter, we look more closely at business and legal conflicts that can arise in domain name trademark disputes. We also discuss how you can protect yourself from these potential problems by conducting a trademark search after you register your domain name. You discover how to conduct a trademark search yourself and how to use an online search service, a trademark firm, or a trademark attorney. We also take a look at organizations you can turn to for additional information and assistance.

We aren't providing any legal advice. We're simply pointing out possible trademark pitfalls and letting you know how you can protect yourself by gathering important information before you start using your domain name in your business. The more you know, the more you will be able to protect yourself against future problems.

What Is a Trademark?

A trademark can be a word, a name, a symbol, or any combination that is used, for commercial purposes, to set one seller apart from its competitors. Whether they are business names, product names, or logos, trademarks enable consumers to identify the source of goods.

In the United States, trademark holders can be protected by three different types of trademark rights:

- **Federal trademark rights:** These rights may apply to trademarks that are used in commerce across state, territorial, or national borders.

- **State trademark rights:** These may apply to trademarks used only within the borders of a state.

- **Common-law trademark rights:** These rights may arise merely from being the first to use a trademark and employing it in commerce for more than a year.

We look more closely at these different kinds of trademark rights throughout this chapter. In the following sections, we consider two key principles of trademark law.

Federal registration of trademarks

In most cases, no matter what the trademark conflict, a party who registered her name or mark as a United States federal or state trademark usually has stronger, broader rights than someone whose name or mark has not been registered (unless common-law rights, covered later in this section, come into play). Federal trademark registration conveys a number of important benefits, including:

- A legal presumption of the mark's ownership and validity

- Greater protection against other marks that are similar in sound, appearance, and meaning

- Exclusive rights to use the mark in accordance with the terms of its registration

✔ Potential adjudication of trademark conflicts in federal court

✔ The ability to ask the United States Customs Service to block the importation of infringing products into this country

The bottom line is that if you obtain federal trademark registration of your domain name, it becomes much easier for you to win any trademark infringement lawsuits. With registration, the presumption of the law is on your side, and you are entitled to the mark's legal and exclusive use. Perhaps even more important is the fact that others will discover that you have federal trademark rights when they research a similar name. Most people will respect those trademark rights and avoid using a similar or potentially conflicting name.

Although registering your trademark with the United States government enhances your ownership rights, keep in mind that registration by itself does not create those rights. Trademark rights arise by using a name in commerce, and they last only so long as that use persists. (You can also obtain trademark rights by filing an "Intent-to-Use" application, which we'll discuss in Chapter 8.) Just because you have not federally registered your domain name does not mean that you do not have rights. If you are the first to use your domain name in commerce and have employed it for more than a year, building up business goodwill, you acquire the common-law rights, which are enforceable in federal court, to:

✔ Win damages for any harm caused you by an infringing mark

✔ Win punitive damages and legal fees if you can demonstrate that the infringement was intentional

Although common-law rights are more limited than United States federal trademark rights, they do convey a significant measure of protection against other marks that are similar in sound, appearance, or meaning.

Trademarking domain names

In recent years, the courts have recognized that domain names can function as trademarks, and the United States Patent and Trademark Office (PTO) now accepts trademark registrations for domain names (we look more closely at the U.S. Patent and Trademark Office in Chapter 8). It is important to realize, however, that you cannot trademark a domain name that you're simply using as an Internet address. As always in trademark law, use in commerce is the key. In order to qualify as a trademark, a domain name must:

✔ Be used to direct customers to a Web site that commercially offers specific goods or services

✔ Serve as the trade name of a business that sells services or products on the Web

Applying established trademark law to domain names has been tricky, however. In the real world, state, federal, and international trademark status is defined by geographic boundaries or marketing territories. Those distinctions disappear on the Web, where, in some ways, there is no such thing as a "local business."

Even if you operate a local bookstore, and the vast majority of your customers come from the surrounding area, as soon as you put up a Web site, your offerings become available to customers across the country and across the globe. You may be the only Bertram's Bookstore in Flint, Michigan, but it is likely that there are hundreds of companies named Bertram's around the world, and your domain name may bring you into a trademark conflict with one or more of them.

Domain name trademark disputes are a bit difficult to examine, because many of the cases have been settled confidentially, making it hard to establish clear patterns of liability. In most domain name trademark infringement and dilutions disputes, however, three standards are generally used to weigh competing trademark rights:

- ✔ **Fame.** If the mark is famous, it will probably be found to have stronger rights.

- ✔ **Confusion.** If neither of the conflicting marks is famous, liability hinges on a mark's likelihood of causing customer confusion.

- ✔ **First come, first served.** Whoever used the name or mark in commerce first has greater rights.

Rules for domain name trademark disputes can be hard to pin down internationally as well. Traditionally, a trademark exists independently in each country in which it is registered. For example, two companies called Marilla — one in Switzerland and the other in the United States — can both exist and hold separate trademarks in their respective countries. The Swiss Marilla, however, cannot market its goods in the United States under that business name, and similar restrictions would apply to the American company if it sought to sell its goods or services in Switzerland.

If the Swiss company registers Marilla.com on the Internet, however, and sets up a commercial Web site, those traditional boundaries and distinctions break down. Which company has the strongest rights to that address? Courts and arbitration centers such as ICANN and the World Intellectual Property Organization (WIPO) are attempting to sort out those issues (see Chapter 7 for more details).

Avoiding Trademarked Names

Because trademark owners frequently take action against people who infringe on their trademark rights, you need to be sure to choose a business domain name that does not conflict with any trademark rights. After all, ignorance is no protection in the eyes of the law. Even if you had no idea that the domain name you registered and put to use was infringing on another's mark, you can be forced to forfeit the name and all the goodwill that has been associated with it.

Going with a generic name

How do you avoid choosing a conflicting Internet address? One approach is to opt for a *generic* domain name made up of common dictionary words that are synonymous with the commercial product you are offering, such as *flowers* for floral services, *candy* for an online sweets shop, and *pillows* for a bedding supplier. The law does not permit these words to be trademarked when they are paired with the goods or services they obviously describe. As a result, these words, used alone or in combination in the creation of domain names, are usually a safe choice in terms of avoiding trademark conflicts.

Unfortunately, for these reasons, generic domain names have also been snapped up fast by many registrants, and they command relatively high values on the resale market. For example, Procter & Gamble registered more than 100 such domain names related to consumer goods categories, including Dandruff.com, Badbreath.com, Underarm.com, Beautiful.com, Clean.com, Condition.com, Dry.com, Flu.com, Romantic.com, Thirst.com, and Sensitive.com.

The downside of domain names like these is that, because they cannot be trademarked, they can also be difficult for a business to protect. As the Internet marketplace evolves, the pros and cons of generic domain names will probably become clearer.

Where to go for trademark help

Trademark issues can be complex and confusing, but resources are available to give you valuable information and assistance. They include the following:

✔ **International Trademark Association (INTA),** 1133 Avenue of the Americas, New York, NY 10036; phone: 212-768-9887; fax: 212-768-7796; Web site: www.inta.org.

✔ **The Sunnyvale Center on Innovation, Invention and Ideas,** 465 South Mathilda Avenue, Suite 300, Sunnyvale, CA 94086; phone: 408-730-7290; Web site: www.sci3.com.

✔ **The U.S. Patent and Trademark Office (PTO) PTO Trademark Assistance Center,** phone: 800-786-9199 (the best phone numbers for advice are 703-308-9000 and 703-308-HELP); Web site: www.uspto.gov.

The famous British rock star Sting found out first-hand about the elusive trademark qualities of generic names. Sting wanted the domain name Sting.com, which had been used for eight years by its U.S. registrant. Even though Sting is a celebrity, the court ruled against him because the word *sting* is a common English word. Moreover, Sting is not the musician's real name, which is Gordon Sumner, and no bad faith had been involved. On the other hand, a generic word can be used as a trademark in different contexts. For example, the word "Apple" would be considered generic for apple producers and could not be trademarked in that case; however, "Apple" could be used as a trademark for computer brands or music labels. In a recent case, Crew.com was found to infringe upon the J.Crew clothing company's trademark, despite the overall generic nature of the word "crew."

In one case, the use of the letter *e* in front of a generic word resulted in trademark protection. The Californian company E-Stamp Corp. registered and obtained a trademark for the brand name E-Stamp, and it registered the domain names E-stamp.com and Estamp.com. In June 2000, the company filed a lawsuit for trademark infringement against an individual who had registered the domain names Estamps.com and E-stamps.com, along with more than 100 other domain names. Even though the defendant argued that the word *e-stamp* is generic and does not have trademark protection, the U.S. District Court Judge ruled that E-Stamp is a unique name. The defendant was forced to turn over the infringing domain names to E-Stamp.

Conducting a trademark search

To protect yourself from potential trademark problems, the best thing you can do, in addition to registering a generic domain name, is to conduct some trademark research as soon as you register your domain name. The process for discovering potential conflicts is called a trademark search, and it is a step that you should take before using your domain name in commerce.

Why is it necessary to do this kind of research? Because, unfortunately, domain name registrars do not research federal, state, and common-law trademarks before they make domain names available to registrants. All they search is the domain name registry to make sure that someone else has not already claimed a domain name with that exact spelling. Therefore, you're the one responsible for conducting a trademark search. Performing this due diligence is well worth the extra effort if you plan to invest your new domain name, time, money, and reputation in a business.

Another important factor to consider is that the failure to conduct a comprehensive trademark search before you begin using your domain name in commerce can be used as evidence that you deliberately infringed on another's mark — especially if you had reason to believe in the existence of the other trademark. For all these reasons, clearing your domain names of conflicts before you use it in your business is a prudent and legally responsible step to take.

When you conduct a trademark search, there are three research areas to look at:

- ✔ **The United States Federal Trademark Register.** This database lets you know if there are any federally registered marks that could potentially conflict with your domain name in sound, appearance, or meaning.

- ✔ **State trademark registrations.** Although state trademark holders have more limited rights than federal trademarks registrants, a conflicting state trademark could prevent you from using your domain name in that particular state — a serious problem for a business that markets nationally and globally on the Net.

- ✔ **The World Wide Web, publications, product, and service announcements, and other sources.** All of these resources can turn up similar *common-law* trademarks — unregistered marks that have already been used in commerce and that may prevent you from using your potentially conflicting domain name.

You can contact the U.S. Patent and Trademark Office at Crystal Park 3, Suite 461, Washington, DC 20231; fax: 703-306-2662; Web site: www.uspto.gov. You can find a list of local Patent and Trademark Depository Libraries at www.uspto.gov/web/offices/ac/ido/ptdl/ptdlib_1.html.

You can also access the federal trademark database online through TESS, the PTO's Trademark Electronic Search System, at tess.uspto.gov. Although TESS enables you to search federal marks yourself for free and can be a good place to start, it is not the most up-to-date or user-friendly of search systems. Plus, the PTO does not provide you with any information about state or common-law trademarks.

For an easier, more comprehensive trademark search, you may want to consider using one of the online search services available from a variety of trademark service companies. Using these search services, you can get a quick sense of whether your domain name conflicts directly with any federal marks. If, for example, this type of search turns up a likely similarity or conflict, you will know that you should probably find another domain name rather than investing more time and money in a more extensive search. Sometimes called a *knock out* or *direct hit* search, this type of screening is the first step in clearing your domain name of potential trademark conflicts.

Several companies offer online trademark screening:

- ✔ **MarksOnline** (www.marksonline.com) provides a free preliminary search of United States registered federal trademarks.

- ✔ **NameProtect** (www.nameprotect.com) checks your domain name against complete U.S. and Canadian trademark registries, searching for any mark that a consumer may confuse with your domain name. NameProtect offers a free, preliminary online, real-time screening search, as well as more comprehensive search capabilities, using a simple interface designed for non-search professionals.

If you find a direct hit conflict in one of these screening searches, the results will list the number of conflicts, the type or *International Class* of business, and the kinds of goods or services it provides. In the event that you do find a conflict, it means that another business has established trademark rights to the same or similar name. Very likely, you will have a trademark problem on your hands if you decide to go ahead and use the domain name in business.

Ask yourself a number of important questions if you run into a conflict with your domain name and a trademark:

✔ Is there a trademark infringement conflict that the use of my domain name would cause?

✔ Even if it looks like there is no technical violation, is there a risk that a trademark holder will challenge my domain name? And is using the domain name worth the risk?

✔ Is there another company that my potential customers may confuse with my business — and could this potentially cause me problems?

If you are not convinced that you should give up your potentially conflicting domain name, you may want to consult a trademark attorney at this point to get a realistic evaluation of the risks that may be involved in using it.

If, on the other hand, a direct-hit search of federal marks does not turn up any conflicts, take your research another step and do a more comprehensive search of state and common-law trademark resources. With some 2 million federal trademarks, half a million state trademarks, and about 13.5 million common law marks in use, getting the help of a trademark firm to conduct this type of search makes sense. This expanded kind of search is not usually available in real-time, because it generally requires the efforts of a trademark research specialist. Still, many trademark companies make it easy for you to order these expanded searches online, and some provide next-day results.

A variety of trademark search firms provide comprehensive search services, ranging in price from $175 to $750 per domain name. Although using these search firms can add up to a substantial amount of money, keep in mind that it is an investment you need to make in order to protect your business from potential future lawsuits and business interruptions, which could prove far more costly. Search firms also generally charge less for these services than do trademark attorneys, who may charge as much as $2,000 for a comprehensive trademark search.

Trademark firms that provide comprehensive search capabilities include:

✔ **1-2-3 Trademark** (www.1-2-3-trademark.com) provides direct-hit federal trademark screening, in-depth searches of state and federal databases for exact or similar trademark conflicts, and full searches of United States common-law records, including corporation and limited partnership filings, business and corporate Information, "Doing Business As" Filings, franchise databases, and fictitious business name information.

✔ **4TradeMark.com** (`www.trademark-search.com`) offers direct-hit federal database searches for a fee; comprehensive searches of federal, state, and common-law sources; and Canadian trademark searches.

✔ **NameProtect** (`www.nameprotect.com`) offers comprehensive search services, including hundreds of state trademark databases and common-law sources, including brand and business name directories and yellow pages. A trained researcher completes the search in about four business days and provides a fully documented report booklet detailing your results.

✔ **Trademark Center** (`www.tmcenter.com`) offers a screening search of the Federal Trademark Register for a fee, as well as expanded searches of federal, state, and common-law sources, including databases of more than 10 million public and private U.S. businesses. The most comprehensive search looks for marks that may conflict directly with your domain name as well as marks that have a similar sound, appearance, or meaning.

✔ **Trademark Express** (`www.trademarkexpress.com`) offers comprehensive trademark and common-law searches, including research of international trade names and logo designs, with free consultations before you search. Service is same-day, and attorneys are available free for reviewing similarities.

When you complete your trademark searches, don't be surprised if you find out that your domain name is uncomfortably close to another existing mark. Unfortunately, it happens all the time. But knowing that before you start using a domain name is certainly better than finding out after you have invested substantial amounts of time and money in an Internet address you plan to use for business purposes.

Coping with Critics and Competitors

If you are fortunate and your trademark search results show that your domain name is free of potential trademark problems, there are a few other steps that you should consider taking in order to protect it. One is to register your domain as a federal trademark (we look closely at that process in Chapter 8). Another step is to register a number of variations and misspellings as domain names. This strategy can reduce the chances that a competitor will attempt to tarnish or take advantage of your business domain name in the marketplace.

Taking offensive variations off the market

Unlike cybersquatters, many individuals who register similar but not identical domain names do so to criticize businesses or people they dislike. For example, during the 2000 presidential campaign, the Internet address `www.gwbush.com` took you not to George W. Bush's official Web site but to a site that satirized the 2000 Republican candidate. Other critics have launched sites using variations of domain names belonging to companies including McDonald's, Wal-Mart, and United Airlines.

These critical Web sites may enjoy First Amendment free speech protections, and many companies that have considered taking them to court have changed their minds — and their tactics — in the face of public criticism. For example, Verizon — the nation's largest telephone company — threatened to bring a lawsuit against a small company that had registered the domain name VerizonReallySucks.com. Ultimately, however, Verizon backed off, recognizing the free speech implications of the case. It is impossible to predict the outcome of these cases, however. In some ICANN-related arbitration hearings, for example, registrants have lost domain names that were seemingly protected by First Amendment issues.

When a critic of Ford Motor Company launched a Web site that disparaged the carmaker and posted new product information, Ford brought a lawsuit to shut it down. A judge, however, ruled against Ford, declaring that the free speech rights of the Web site publisher should be protected.

Despite the free speech issues, reducing the likelihood of critical sites by proactively registering unflattering variations can be a wise move. United Parcel Service, for example, has registered domain names including UPSstinks.com, IHateUPS.com, and UPSBites.com. Chase Manhattan has registered the domain names IhateChase.com, ChaseStinks.com, ChaseBlows.com, and ChaseSucks. com. Volvo has registered Volvo-sucks.com. And Wal-Mart has registered more than 200 potentially derogatory domain names.

So think about possible variations of your business domain name that somebody may use to undermine you on the Net. Go ahead and register them if they are available. Of course, you can never make it impossible for someone to criticize your business, but you do not have to make it easier than it has to be. After all, your business domain name is your online identity. Consider doing whatever it take to protect it, whether that means making sure it is free of trademark conflicts or reducing the chance of unflattering references.

Registering common misspellings

Consider registering misspellings of your domain name. If your Internet address is Widgeteria.com, for example, you should think about registering Wigeteria.com and Wigiteria.com — not only to direct poor spellers to your site, but also to keep others from using those names to divert potential customers from your business.

Working with a trademark attorney

If a comprehensive trademark search reveals similar names or marks, you have two choices: Discard the domain name and choose another, or contact a trademark attorney for some specialized legal advice. In some cases, of course, you may want to consider using an attorney to conduct a trademark search. If so, the fees will usually range from $750 to $2,000.

Of course, if you're involved in a domain name trademark dispute, you need to get the advice of an experienced trademark attorney. Many trademark search firms have referral networks of attorneys who can help you.

One individual in Pennsylvania, for example, registered the domain names Wallstreetjounal.com and Wallstreetjournel.com — misspellings or typos of WallStreetJournal.com, an Internet address that belongs to Dow Jones & Company — in order to capture *Wall Street Journal* visitors who had made a spelling error. Dow Jones brought a complaint to the World Intellectual Property Organization (WIPO), and WIPO arbitrators ruled that the domain names should be transferred to Dow Jones.

Chapter 7

Dealing with Domain Name Trademark Issues

· ·

In This Chapter

▶ Understanding trademark rights

▶ Resolving trademark disputes

▶ Being familiar with the Anticybersquatting Consumer Protection Act

▶ Looking at international domain name trademark issues

· ·

*I*f you plan to use your domain name for business purposes, registering the domain name is only the first step you need to take. The next important step is making sure that the domain name you have registered is free of potential trademark conflicts. If you use a domain name that does have trademark conflicts, you could end up losing it or paying heavy fines to defend your right to keep it.

Trademark conflict is the hottest area of dispute in the domain name marketplace today. Courts are struggling to define how trademark laws apply on the Internet — a global medium for which they were never designed. In fact, the very nature of the Internet defies some of the traditional legal trademark principles.

In the real world, for example, it is possible for one business name — such as Acme — to apply to several kinds of enterprises, so long as they don't compete with one another and there is no chance that consumers will be confused. In the virtual world, however, there can only be one Acme.net, Acme.org, or Acme.com. Who has the right to that domain name, and what legal issues are involved in obtaining those rights? Those issues are the subjects of numerous heated battles in the courts.

Domain name trademark issues are complicated even more because the Internet and domain name system are worldwide in nature. Given the different trademark laws in different countries, the challenge of protecting and enforcing trademarks on the Internet is complex, and it is an area where things are currently much less black-and-white than other aspects of the law.

Nothing in this and other chapters in this book should be construed as legal advice. Trademark rules differ from place to place. The information here is of general nature only, and should not be used in place of consulting with an attorney experienced in this field of law.

In the early days, the Internet was, to a considerable extent, a Wild West environment, where few, if any, legal rules seemed to apply. Courts and legislators are now trying to tame the Web's legal free-for-all, coming down hard on some of the most questionable practices. One notorious domain name issue is known as *cybersquatting* — registering a domain name that infringes on someone else's trademark with the deliberate intent to profit unfairly from that Internet address. Cybersquatters can now face serious financial penalties, according to new federal legislation signed into law by the President in November 1999. New arbitration processes were also established in 1999 to bring some order to the confusion regarding conflicting trademark rights in cyberspace and to address the issue of cybersquatters directly.

In this chapter, we take a look at some of the basic concepts in trademark laws that are relevant to domain names, the perils of cybersquatting, and some elements of new laws and arbitration processes created to resolve domain name trademark disputes. Although this chapter does not offer any legal advice, it does begin to explore some issues that should be of concern to anyone who is participating in the domain name marketplace.

Knowing Who Has the Rights to a Domain Name

Because domain names are unique Internet addresses that also serve as brand names in the online marketplace, domain name trademark conflicts have become more and more common, especially as the number of registered domain names has skyrocketed. Trademark disputes can arise whenever two or more individuals, organizations, or businesses claim rights to the same or similar domain names. They are particularly likely to come up in situations like these:

- ✔ **Identical business names.** For example, a gumball manufacturer and a sports equipment company may both use the business name "Wonderball," and both want to use the domain name Wonderball.com on the Web.

- ✔ **Similar names.** The domain name 4-movies.com, for example, may be confusingly similar in sound, appearance, or meaning to other domain names such as 4movies.com and Formovies.com

- ✔ **Conflicting acronyms.** A Cleveland law firm called Kelly Martin Mitchell, for example, wants to use the domain name KMM.com — but so does the KMM stationery store in Mesa, Arizona.

✔ **International disputes.** For instance, a Parisian restaurant and a Seattle coffee company both use the business name Café du Monde, and both want to use the domain name Cafedumonde.com.

✔ **Famous names.** A celebrity, for example, wants to use her name as the address for an official Web site for her fans — but someone has already registered her name as a domain name and is asking for a huge amount of money to sell it back to her.

This is an example of cybersquatting, a practice that is now illegal, provided that it can be demonstrated that the cybersquatter registered the domain name in question in "bad faith." Cybersquatting victims can now pursue remedies in court or bring their complaint to an arbitration panel approved by the Internet Corporation for Assigned Names and Numbers (ICANN) for judgment under its new dispute resolution policy (we look more closely at both of these options later in this chapter).

Taking a Brief Tour through Trademark Law

To understand why trademark issues have gotten so complex, you need to understand some of the basic concepts of trademark law. (Don't worry, we keep it simple.) Traditionally, trademark law has been used to settle disputes between businesses that use confusingly similar marks (names, numbers, words, logos, colors, unique aromas, sounds, and the like). The purpose of trademark law is to prevent consumers from being confused about which business is the source of which products and services offered in the marketplace. The laws also exist to keep businesses from taking unfair advantage of the reputation and goodwill that other companies have legitimately established with consumers.

In the real, physical, brick-and-mortar world, it is perfectly possible for two companies with the same business name to exist if they avoid confusion by selling different goods or services, if they market those products in different geographical areas, or if they sell them through different types of distribution channels or to completely different types of customers. For example, there can be a TipTop Dry Cleaners and a TipTop Food Distributors in Iowa. In this case, the name TipTop is not likely to cause customer confusion, since customers can easily tell the difference between the dry cleaners and the food distributor.

Trademark conflicts arise, however, when business names or marks are likely to mislead customers or confuse them about which company is the actual provider of the goods and services they're looking for. Keep in mind that trademarked names do not have to be identical to cause confusion. A bakery called Drink 'n Doughnuts, for example, may have a trademark problem on its hands if it is challenged by the national bakery chain Dunkin' Donuts. And the more famous a trademark is, the more its owners can claim that others with similar — but not identical — names are violating their trademark rights.

Trademark law and the Internet

Trademark issues get a lot more complicated on the Internet, where geographic boundaries disappear and only one `.com` domain name is available for every business name, no matter how many companies in different industries and places use it. Plus, in the virtual, borderless world of cyberspace, trademark issues get even more complex when you consider the *international* trademark implications. Imagine, for example, three companies that use the business name Autoplus — one in the United States, one in France, and one in Australia. Who owns the trademark rights to the domain name on the Internet, given the fact that there can be only one Autoplus.com?

This new commercial environment is testing trademark laws that were designed for the physical, bricks-and-mortar world. As one judge explained it, "Attempting to apply established trademark law in the fast-moving world of the Internet is like trying to board a moving bus." Nevertheless, the courts are slowly beginning to establish some legal ground rules. Here are a few questions that today generally govern trademark conflicts on the Net:

- ✔ **Is the domain name so similar to another name or trademark that it is likely to confuse potential customers?** For example, the domain names 4-movies.com and Formovies.com may be spelled differently, but they sound identical. A potential customer may easily be confused, especially when hearing an advertisement for the services on the radio.

- ✔ **Is the domain name similar to a well-known trademark? If so, it could be challenged by the owner of the famous mark?** In these cases, it is not necessary for the famous trademark owner to prove that customer confusion is probable. For example, customers probably wouldn't confuse the Exxon brand name with a Web site using the domain name Exxoff.com, which sells products and services to discount gas stations. But there is a good chance that that Web site owner would find herself, at the very least, with a cease-and-desist letter on her hands.

Essentially, trademark law is designed to prevent unfair business practices. Under the Lanham Act (the federal statute that governs United States trademark law), the intentional use of someone else's trademark is considered a form of unfair competition, a cardinal sin in the world of business. According to trademark law, several types of commercial practices constitute unfair competition. Two of the most important are trademark infringement and trademark dilution, which we cover in more detail in the following sections.

Trademark infringement

Any unauthorized use of a trademarked name or mark may constitute trademark infringement. One name or mark infringes on another when it is likely to confuse or mislead customers. To win an infringement case, a trademark holder does not have to show that confusion actually occurred — only that it is reasonably likely.

When weighing competing claims in a trademark infringement case, a judge will usually consider:

- ✔ Which party actually owns the trademark
- ✔ Who first registered the mark
- ✔ Who was the first to use it in commerce

Domain names can be — and have been — challenged for trademark infringement violations. If the holder of a domain name loses an infringement suit, he may be forced to forfeit the right to the name or may be prevented from using it — an inconvenient and potentially expensive prospect. Even worse, the domain name registrant may also be liable for damages.

A heated battle over domain name trademark infringement was waged by the online retailer eToys.com against a Zurich-based artists' Web site with the domain name Etoy.com. The Etoy.com domain name was in use two years *before* the retailer eToys registered its domain name as a U.S. federal trademark. Even so, a Superior Court judge in Los Angeles ruled in favor of the retailer, agreeing that its trademark was being violated by the artists' group, whose work occasionally included profanity and nudity. As a result, the Zurich Web site was shut down — but eToys suffered so much criticism for its action that it decided to reach a settlement with the artists' group.

Trademark dilution

Unlike trademark infringement, claims of trademark dilution are reserved for famous trademarks — brand names such as Exxon or Microsoft. A company may win a dilution claim without proving probable customer confusion. All that is necessary is to show that the conflicting name simply dilutes or tarnishes the famous mark's unique and distinctive qualities. Famous trademarks are usually protected vigorously because their value can be huge. The brand name Coca-Cola, for example, accounts for 59 percent of the company's value, according to one study by the Interbrand branding consulting agency.

As a result, domain name registrants are better off steering clear of any name that even remotely resembles a famous trademark. Even if your business is entirely different from a famous trademark holder's, avoid using a similar domain name at all costs. There is little chance, for example, that a domain name like Disneypies.com would go unchallenged, even if the business owner is a baker whose last name is Disney.

Trademark dilution claims have been actively enforced on the Internet. In the case of *Hasbro v. Internet Entertainment Group,* for example, a Seattle company had to stop using the domain name Candyland.com for its adult-oriented Web site because Candyland is a well-known children's board game marketed by Hasbro. Although consumers would not be confused by the use of the name, the court agreed with Hasbro that use of its well-known trademark as a porn site would likely diminish the value and goodwill that was associated with their mark.

One of the very first domain name trademark conflicts occurred when a reporter registered the domain name Mcdonalds.com after discovering that McDonald's Corporation had not claimed it. The reporter published an article using the domain name in *Wired* magazine. McDonald's Corporation took action to get its domain name from the reporter. He agreed to surrender it to them in exchange for a donation to a New York City school.

One of the all-time biggest domain name lawsuits involved trademark dilution issues. In the spring of 2000, The organizers of the Olympic Games filed a federal lawsuit to stop the use of 1,800 domain names registered to individuals in 54 different countries. The names infringed on various Olympic trademarks, including misspellings and words in a variety of languages.

Trademark and domain name conflicts

Trademark conflicts have become increasingly common as many traditional companies and organizations decide, at a late date, to develop a presence on the Internet. Many of them discover, to their dismay, that others have already registered their domain names, often for legitimate reasons. Depending on the situation, companies may go to great lengths and apply great legal pressure on the domain name holder to obtain the rights to the Internet address they seek. For many legitimate domain name owners who find themselves the target of these efforts, giving up their domain name may be cheaper than fighting the matter in court. This unfortunate phenomenon has become known as "reverse domain name hijacking."

In some cases, companies avoid litigation by making a financial settlement with the owner of the domain name they are challenging. A number of years ago, for example, the Potato Growers of Alberta registered its initials as the domain name PGA.com. Those initials also happen to stand for the Professional Golfers' Association — and when the golfers' group decided that it wanted that domain name, it convinced the potato growers to turn it over, for a fee.

When Archie Comics, creator of the Veronica character, discovered that the domain name Veronica.org had already been registered, its lawyers threatened to sue the domain name holder for trademark infringement. The target of its threats was a father who had innocently registered the domain name to set up a Web site for his 22-month-old daughter, Veronica. Under the threat of legal action, the father chose to shut down his daughter's site. Still, even though large, well-funded companies often go after domain name holders they believe are violating their well-known trademarks, they don't always win. In one case, for example, a 12-year-old boy who was nicknamed "Pokey" registered the domain name Pokey.org. Now, Pokey — along with Gumby — is also the name of a famous toy and animated character whose trademark is owned by the Prema Toy Company. When Prema tried to take the boy's domain name away, the company suffered so much public criticism that it dropped its attempts to claim the domain name.

In another case, two jazz music clubs — both called The Blue Note — found themselves in a domain name trademark dispute even though one was located in New York City and the other in Columbia, Missouri. A New York federal court judge decided against the famous New York City club and in favor of the small-town nightspot, which had put up a Web site using the domain name it had registered, Thebluenote.com.

Trademark issues to consider

Unfortunately, trademark law has very few bright lines — and a lot of gray areas — especially concerning its application on the Internet.

If you think there might be a chance of customer confusion, here are some issues to consider before you decide whether to use a potentially conflicting domain name in commerce (or whether to try to acquire an already acquired domain name you think you're entitled to):

- ✔ **First come, first served.** This rule frequently applies to trademarks. The first to use a domain name or a trademark in commerce has stronger legal rights to use the name in that geographic area than other businesses offering similar goods or services.

- ✔ **Use it or lose it.** The wider the geographic area in which a trademark is used — and the longer the time that it is used in commerce — the stronger, in general, are its trademark rights. In fact, to establish trademark rights, commercial use is all that is required. By the same token, you can lose your trademark rights if you stop using a trademark in commerce for a long period of time, usually one or two years. After all, if it is not used in the marketplace, the purpose of a trademark — to help distinguish one seller of goods and services from another — no longer exists.

- ✔ **Degree of confusion.** How probable is it that customers would be confused? Have there been any actual instances when customer confusion has occurred?

- ✔ **Bad faith.** Did the owner of the potentially conflicting domain name or trademark deliberately attempt to confuse or mislead customers or take advantage of the other company's reputation in the marketplace?

- ✔ **Right to use.** Are you legitimately entitled to use the name?

If a domain name is likely to cause confusion, if it came into use after a similar name or trademark, and especially if it is being used in bad faith, there is a significant chance that the person who owns that domain name (and that may be you) will lose his rights to continue using that name and may be found liable for damages incurred.

Recognizing the Perils of Cybersquatting

The most notorious examples of domain name holders operating in bad faith or violating famous trademarks are cases of cybersquatting. Cybersquatters are people who deliberately register the names of celebrities or the trademarks of famous companies, denying the rightful owner access to the domain name, in the hopes of selling the names back to their rightful owners (or the highest bidder) for large amounts of money.

Some cybersquatters — especially in the early days of the Web — got away with the practice. Like many companies, for example, MTV neglected to register the domain name MTV.com early on. Seeing a potentially profitable opportunity, one of its former employees registered the MTV.com domain name first, then sold it back to the TV network for around $1 million.

Other cybersquatters have been less lucky. One cybersquatting pioneer in Illinois, for instance, registered more than 240 domain names based on famous trademarks, including Yankeestadium.com, Deltaairlines.com, Neimanmarcus.com, and others. When the trademark owners asked him to give up the names so that they could use them, he demanded large amounts of money in exchange. Ultimately, the cybersquatter ended up with a federal lawsuit against him for trademark dilution and lost ownership of his domain names.

 Cybersquatters do not have to register the exact spelling of a famous name or trademark to run afoul of the courts. A Miami businessman, for example, registered the domain name Wwwpainewebber.com — just one dot away from Pain Webber's actual Internet address, `www.painewebber.com`. A federal court in the state of Virginia issued an injunction prohibiting him from continuing to use the name.

If, unfortunately, you do find yourself in a domain name dispute — especially one involving cybersquatting — it will likely be settled or resolved in one of two arenas: a federal lawsuit or an arbitration process created by ICANN. We take a look at both of these options in the following sections.

The Anticybersquatting Consumer Protection Act

One new remedy for people and companies who have been victims of domain name cybersquatting is new legislation passed by Congress in 1999. The Anticybersquatting Consumer Protection Act in 1999 amends the Trademark Act of 1946 to enable trademark or service mark owners to sue, for civil damages, anyone who registers, traffics in, or uses a domain name with a bad faith intent to profit from the trademark.

If you want to bring a claim under the Anticybersquatting Act, you need to file a federal court lawsuit. A domain holder who is found guilty of cybersquatting under the act may be ordered to forfeit or cancel the domain name or transfer it to the trademark owner. In addition, the guilty party may be liable for statutory damages ranging from $1,000 to $100,000 per domain name.

The Anticybersquatting Consumer Protection Act applies to domain names that are:

- ✔ **Identical or confusingly similar to a distinctive mark**.

- ✔ **Dilutive of a famous trademark.** This includes protected trademarks, words, or names. (We cover more on trademark dilution in Chapter 6.)

As with the ICANN policy, the Anticybersquatting Consumer Protection Act requires a demonstration that a domain name was registered, trafficked in, or used in bad faith. Factors to be considered under the act include:

- ✔ **The domain name registrant's trademark rights to the domain name.**

- ✔ **The legal or commonly used name of the domain name holder and whether the domain name consists of that name.**

- ✔ **Commercial use of the domain name.**

- ✔ **Noncommercial or fair use of the trademark in a Web site using the domain name.**

- ✔ **Intention to confuse and divert customers from the trademark owner's Web site to another site, using the domain name, that could harm the trademark holder's reputation.**

- ✔ **Cybersquatting, or attempting to transfer or sell the domain name to the rightful trademark owner or another party for financial gain without having any intention to use the domain name in a legitimate, commercial manner.**

> ✔ The use of misleading, false contact information when registering the domain name, as well as intentional failure to maintain accurate contact information.

> ✔ Deliberate infringement by knowingly registering or acquiring multiple domain names that are identical or confusingly similar to distinctive trademarks held by others or dilutive of the famous trademarks of others.

Although the Anticybersquatting Consumer Protection Act applies to all domain names, no matter when they were registered, complainants can only seek damages for domain names that were registered after November 2, 1999. For domain names registered before that date, complainants can seek injunctive relief and the transfer of rights to the domain name.

The first appellate ruling under the Anticybersquatting Consumer Protection Act involved a case called *Sporty's Farm v. Sportsman's Market Inc.* In that ruling, the U.S. Court of Appeals for the Second Circuit found that a Christmas tree company called Sporty's Farm had registered the domain name Sportys.com in bad faith and ordered it to turn the domain name over to the Sporty's trademark holder, Sportsman's Market, Inc. Sportsman's Market is an aviation and tool catalog company that has traditionally used — and federally trademarked — the name Sporty's for its products.

Arbitration by ICANN

Another new vehicle for resolving domain name trademark conflicts is ICANN's new Uniform Domain Name Dispute Resolution Policy, which is being voluntarily adopted and implemented by all ICANN-accredited domain name registrars of the .com, .net, and .org gTLDS as well ccTLD registrars. The new policy applies to domain names registered since January 1, 2000, and it focuses on disputes involving these bad faith trademark issues:

> ✔ **Cybersquatting:** Registering a domain name in order to prevent the rightful trademark owner from using it, or for the purpose of selling, renting, or transferring it to the rightful trademark owner or a competitor for more than out-of-pocket costs.

> ✔ **Customer confusion:** Using a domain name intentionally to confuse and attract Internet users for commercial gain.

> ✔ **Ill will:** Registering a domain name primarily for the purpose of disrupting the business of a competitor.

The ICANN policy applies to domain name registrants who have:

> ✔ A domain name that is identical or confusingly similar to a trademark or service mark in which the complaining party has rights.

✔ No rights or legitimate interests in the disputed domain name.

✔ A domain name that has been registered and is being used in bad faith.

If you file a complaint against a domain name holder in an administrative ICANN proceeding, you must prove each of these three elements in order to win your case.

If you are a trademark owner and want to invoke the ICANN policy against a domain name holder, you can either file a complaint in court or submit it to one of ICANN's four approved dispute-resolution service providers. (*Note:* Telephone and fax numbers for international organizations include the international access code (011) to use when dialing from the United States. No international access code is needed when calling Canada from the United States.)

CPR Institute for Dispute Resolution
366 Madison Avenue
New York, NY 10017
Telephone: 212-949-6490
Fax: 212-949-8859
E-mail: icann@cpradr.org
Web site: www.cpradr.org

eResolution
4200 St-Laurent, Bureau 711
Montreal, Quebec
Canada H2W 2R2
Telephone: 514-908-2900
Fax: 514-908-2901
E-mail: info@eresolution.com
Web site: www.eresolution.ca

The National Arbitration Forum
P.O. Box 50191
Minneapolis, MN 55405
Telephone: 800-474-2371
Fax: 651-631-0802
Web site: www.arbforum.com

World Intellectual Property Organization
Arbitration and Mediation Center
34, chemin des Colombettes
P.O. Box 18
1211 Geneva 20
Switzerland
Telephone: (011) 41 22 338 9111
Telefax: (011) 41 22 740 3700
E-mail: arbiter.mail@wipo.int
Web site: arbiter.wipo.int

The cost of filing an ICANN complaint generally runs about $1,000 or less, which is far less than it usually costs to argue such a complaint in court. The process is also faster than litigation. Many cases can be decided within two months, usually based entirely on written materials that have been submitted. No in-person appearance is typically required. If the ICANN-approved arbitrator finds that a domain name holder has met the tests of violating a trademark in bad faith, the domain name registrar will cancel, suspend, or transfer the rights to that domain name. No damage awards are made, and it is possible to appeal the ruling.

Going Global with Trademarks

Although the ICANN policy and the Anticybersquatting Consumer Protection Act are helping to sort out some major trademark conflicts in the United States, the complexity and difficulty of trademark disputes multiplies when you consider the international marketplace. With the worldwide reach of the Internet, domain name trademark issues are clearly international, but no international trademark protection system exists. So who decides who has the right to a domain name held by an American if it infringes on a trademark that was registered in Australia?

To help sort out these issues and create an international forum for resolving global domain name trademark conflicts, ICANN accredited the World Intellectual Property Organization (WIPO) in 1999 to administer international cases under its Uniform Dispute Resolution Policy.

Headquartered in Geneva, Switzerland, the WIPO Arbitration and Mediation Center offers arbitration and mediation services to resolve international commercial disputes between private parties. WIPO procedures have been developed by leading experts in cross-border dispute settlement, and they focus particularly on intellectual property disputes. With more than 800 neutral mediators and arbitrators from over 70 countries, WIPO settles disputes in any language involving parties from any country in the world.

Interestingly, although WIPO is an international organization, most of its cases originate in the United States.

As an alternative to lengthy and expensive international litigation, WIPO attempts to resolve each domain name registration and trademark dispute that it handles quickly and inexpensively within a six-week period, using ICANN's Uniform Domain Name Dispute Resolution Policy (which has also been voluntarily adopted by ICANN-accredited registrars of the international ccTLDs).

By August 2000, WIPO had taken in 1,162 cases. Like other ICANN mediation centers, WIPO has tended to rule in favor of those bringing the complaints. The organization has ordered domain name transfers in 61 percent of cases and denied complaints in just 15 percent.

Some WIPO cases have also attracted controversy. In one instance, the organization ruled that the domain name Wal-MartCanadaSucks.com should be awarded to Wal-Mart — a decision that some criticized for inhibiting free speech about the retail chain.

The French newspaper *Le Monde* turned to WIPO in September 2000 to resolve a conflict over its trademark rights. The domain name Le-monde.com, had been registered by an individual in France who claimed he intended to use it for a Web site. The registrant also pointed out that the words he used in the domain name — *le monde* (which means "the world" in French) — are ordinary, generic, dictionary words that cannot be trademarked. Even so, the WIPO arbitrator ordered him to turn over his domain name to the newspaper *Le Monde*.

When ICANN approves new TLDs, the trademark issues will only become more complex. Who should rightfully own, for example, the domain name Amazon.arts — an art gallery named "Amazon" that may want to register the address or the online superstore Amazon.com? Stay tuned for some heated court and arbitration battles as Internet businesses increasingly attempt to tame the fluid, boundary-free world of cyberspace.

Winners and losers

Although the ICANN dispute resolution policy is attempting to bring some order to a chaotic legal area, it has also drawn its share of criticism, mainly because the majority of its cases have tended to be decided in favor of the trademark owners and companies with deep pockets that initiate the complaints.

For example, a small company called Current Event found itself in a trademark dispute with a bigger company called Current USA over the rights to the domain name Current.com. Current Event had registered the name in 1997 and never knowingly infringed on the trademark rights of Current USA or used the domain name in bad faith. Nevertheless, Current Event lost its right to the domain name through ICANN's dispute resolution process.

Chapter 8

Trademarking Your Domain Name

*A*fter you have determined that your domain name is clear of any potential trademark problems, the best step to take next is to protect it by
submitting it for federal trademark registration. Trademark registration is not
necessary — you can simply begin using your domain name in business and
establish common-law trademark rights by demonstrating first commercial
use. However, by registering your domain name as a federal trademark, you
will gain enhanced legal protections, including:

- The legal presumption that you own the mark
- Protection against future marks that are similar in sound, appearance, or meaning.
- Exclusive rights to use the mark, according to its registration terms
- The ability to bring a trademark infringement or dilution lawsuit in federal court
- The ability to ask the United States Customs Service to block the importation of infringing products
- The ability to win punitive damages for willful infringement.

The key points are these: A federal trademark gives you greater protection —
and, if you find yourself in a trademark dispute, it will shift the balance of
legal presumptions in your favor.

Registering your domain as a federal trademark is not difficult to do, but it can take some time and present a few hurdles along the way. In this chapter, we look closely at the United States Patent and Trademark Office application procedure, discuss what to expect, and share some tips for making the registration process as smooth as possible.

Determining Whether You Can File for a Federal Trademark

You may submit your domain name for federal trademark registration only if you are the registered owner of the domain name (according to the whois database). If you are not the individual to whom the domain name is actually registered, your trademark application will be rejected.

Federal trademark applications may be filed by parties including individuals, corporations, partnerships, or other entities. In the case of domain names, most trademark applicants have traditionally been in the business of computer services and online sales, although the U.S. Patent and Trademark Office (PTO) also receives applications from domain name holders in many other categories of goods and services.

You can only register a domain name as a trademark with the PTO if it is used in interstate commerce — meaning that you use your domain name in a business that provides tangible or intangible products, services, or activities directed to customers across state, territorial, or national boundaries.

How long does a trademark registration last?

Federal trademarks are registered for an indefinite time, as long as they are renewed after five years, ten years, and then every ten years after that.

After your federal trademark registration has been in effect for five years, you must file an "Affidavit of Use" providing certain required information — *between the fifth and sixth year* — or your registration will be canceled.

For an additional fee, you may file the affidavit within a six-month grace period after the end of the sixth year.

To renew your registration for another ten-year period, you need to file a renewal application *between the ninth and tenth year,* before your registration expires. For an extra fee, you can file for renewal within a six-month grace period after the expiration date.

If you use your domain name only for a Web site that advertises your own goods or services, the domain name will not qualify for trademark registration. For example, if you use your domain name Wonderwidgets.com for a Web site that describes your widget products but you do business using a different trademark, you will not be able to seek trademark protection for that name. On the other hand, if you actually conduct online sales of widgets on your Wonderwidgets.com site, your domain name may be federally trademarked, subject to other constraints under trademark law, such as the inability to register descriptive or generic words.

Keep in mind that any commerce associated with your domain name must be bona fide and not performed solely for the purpose of acquiring federal trademark registration.

Figuring Out Whether to File for "Use-Based" or "Intent to Use"

If you have already begun using your domain name in commerce, you can apply for a "use-based" trademark registration. If, on the other hand, you have not begun using your domain name commercially, you have the alternative option of filing an "intent to use" registration. The benefit of filing an "intent to use" is that it dates your trademark application from your filing date — not from the date on which you actually begin using your name. This earlier trademark date can be crucial for establishing your "first come, first served" trademark rights, if you do end up in a conflict with another mark.

If you file an "intent to use" application, you have to agree to use your domain name in bona fide commerce within six months of the date that the PTO approves your application. However, you may purchase up to six additional six-month extensions of that deadline — one at a time for up to three years — for a fee of $150 per extension.

If you do not use your domain name in commerce within the six-month period, and if you do not purchase additional extensions within the acquired extension periods, your federal trademark registration will be abandoned.

Understanding the Trademark Registration Process

Although the trademark registration process is not particularly complicated, it can take a long time — often from ten months to more than two years before you actually receive your trademark registration. The good news is that after you have submitted your trademark application, you begin the process of protecting your domain name and establishing its "first to use" status.

The PTO registration process has five distinct stages. In the following sections, we take a step-by-step look at each of them.

Stage 1: Obtaining an application form

You can get and submit federal trademark application forms in a number of ways. The easiest method is to obtain an application online from the federal Patent and Trademark Office's Trademark Electronic Business Center at www.uspto.gov/web/menu/tmebc/index.html. You can download hard copies of the form at www.uspto.gov/web/forms/index.html#TM.

Knowing special rules for registering domain names

Although domain names are awarded the same federal trademark registrations and rights as any other mark, you should keep in mind some special considerations when you are preparing your PTO application:

✔ **Only the "name" in the domain name can be trademarked.** In other words, if you have a Web site with the URL www.myfirmname.com, only the domain name itself — Myfirmname — is eligible for trademark registration.

✔ **The domain name must be identifiable as the source of goods or services.** This means that customers must identify the Web site by your domain name as the provider of products or services (like Amazon.com or eBay.com are recognized trade names in the marketplace). **Remember:** Simply using your domain name as an Internet address for advertising or an informational Web site is not enough.

✔ **Domain names made up of surnames cannot be trademarked.** For example,

domain names like Wilson.com or Smith.com will not be accepted for trademark registration, unless they have acquired strong market recognition as trademarks.

✔ **Descriptive or generic domain names cannot be trademarked.** For instance, a descriptive name such as Wet.com for a beverage company may not be awarded a federal trademark. In addition, *generic* domain names, made up of ordinary dictionary words, do not qualify. For example, Chicken.com, Shoestore.com, and Weather.com may not be federally trademarked, unless they have acquired strong market recognition as trademarks.

✔ **Geographic descriptions do not qualify.** A domain name that uses a geographic term that is associated with the subject of its service — such as a wine Web site called NapaWines.com — may not be trademarked, unless it has gained strong market recognition.

You can also complete the form online and file electronically at `www.uspto.gov/teas/index.html`. If you choose to file electronically, you must pay the PTO's trademark application fee by credit card.

You may use faxed or photocopied versions of the form, but they must be clean and clear. You may not, however, submit your application by fax.

Stage 2: Submitting your application

In the next step of the trademark registration process, you fill out the form — a procedure that may take as many as three to five hours.

After you've completed the form, follow these steps:

1. **Complete the drawing page for your mark.**

   The federal trademark application requires you to submit a drawing of your name as it will actually appear in commerce. In many cases, a typewritten sample of the domain name is acceptable, following the specific instructions on your trademark application. If you have a logo or logos, you should place them on this page as well.

   Here are some specific guidelines on the application drawing you must provide:

   • **Type of paper.** The drawing must be on pure white, durable, non-shiny, 8½-x-11-inch paper.

   • **Margins.** Keep at least a 1-inch margin on the sides, top, and bottom of the page, and at least 1 inch between the heading and the display of the mark.

   • **Heading.** Include a typewritten heading at the top of the drawing, listing — on separate lines — the complete name and address of the applicant, and the goods and services specified in the application. If you are already using your mark, include the date of its first use anywhere as well as the date of the first use of the mark in interstate commerce.

   • **Capitalization.** If the mark is a typed drawing, the mark must appear in ALL CAPS, like this.

   • **Format.** Place the actual drawing or typewritten sample of your mark in the center of the page.

   In the case of domain names, you can choose whether to include the TLD in your drawing. For example, if your domain name is Widgeteria.com, you can submit a drawing of either *Widgeteria* or *Widgeteria.com*. The TLD makes no material difference to your trademark application. In fact, you can even change the TLD of your domain name — for instance, from Widgeteria.com to Widgeteria.cc — without materially altering your trademark registration or your mark. For most purposes, omitting the TLD is probably more practical.

2. Gather specimens of your mark, as necessary.

If you have already begun using your domain name in commerce and are submitting a "right to use" trademark application, you are also required to submit specimens of how the mark is actually being used in your product or service. The PTO requires one specimen for each class of goods or services that you specify on your application.

Acceptable specimens in the goods categories include labels, tags, or containers for the goods you are providing. You can even send the actual product, if it is not too large or bulky. Acceptable samples of your domain name in the service category include advertisements, brochures, or other materials advertising your specified services. Screen printouts showing use of the mark on your Web site are acceptable as well.

If your specimens are larger than 8½-x-11 inches and do not lie flat, submit a picture clearly showing the mark's use on each specimen instead.

3. Carefully review all the documents in your application package.

Before submitting the form, make sure that you have provided all the information required.

Include a stamped, self-addressed post card listing the mark and the contents of your application package, such as the drawing page, specimens, and a check for the filing fee.

4. Submit your application to the PTO as soon as you have completed it.

Send your completed form to The Assistant Commissioner for Trademarks, Box NEW APP / FEE, 2900 Crystal Drive, Arlington, VA 22202-3513.

If someone else sends in a registration application for the same mark, the PTO will process the application that was filed first.

5. Receive the PTO's confirmation of receipt.

Some time, usually one to three months, after you file for your registration, the PTO looks over your application. If it meets the minimum filing requirements, the examiner sends your self-addressed postcard back to you, stamped with your filing date.

Hang on to the confirmation of receipt, especially your assigned serial number. The serial number identifies your application and should be used on all future correspondence with the PTO.

Within about seven months after you submit your application, the PTO sends you a filing receipt with the serial number of your application, officially notifying you of your filing.

Identification of goods and services

A trademark is only issued for specific goods and/or services. As a result, the trademark application asks you to indicate the actual goods and/or services for which you use — or intend to use — your domain name in commerce. Be as clear, specific, and complete as possible when you state these uses, and avoid general descriptions. For example, if you intend to use your domain name for online sales of venison sausages, you should list "sausages" instead of the general category of "food" or you could specify "Food, including but not limited to venison sausages" if you want to leave the trademark open for future use of other goods and services within that class.

To give you a sense of the degree of specificity that the PTO looks for, here is a sampling of acceptable goods identifications for trademark purposes:

- Abrasive liner for cat litter boxes
- Bumpers for loading docks (rubber)
- Grip tapes for golf clubs
- Missiles (guided)
- V-neck sweaters
- Yucca chips

And here are examples of acceptable service identifications:

- Astrological forecasting
- Cartoon character licensing
- Excursions for tourists (arranging)
- Personal awareness (conducting workshops and seminars in)
- Rental of deep water diving suits
- Wreath making

You can find a complete list of acceptable identifications of goods and services at `www.uspto.gov/web/offices/tac/doc/gsmanual/manual.html`.

Make sure that you list every single product or service for which you want trademark protection, because you will not be able to change your application later to add new items that expand your registration's scope. For example, if your application lists "formal wear rental," you will not be able to change it later to add "clothing alterations." It is easier to narrow the scope of the description of goods rather than to broaden it. That is, when filing the application it is preferable to be overly encompassing and in later stages to delete products and services which you do not provide under the applied-for mark.

 If your application does not meet minimum filing requirements, the PTO will return your entire registration package and filing fee. Filing fees are not normally refundable after your application has been accepted and receives a filing date and serial number.

 Be sure to enclose a check or money order to cover the $325 application fee, and mail your completed form to The Assistant Commissioner for Trademarks, Box NEW APP / FEE, 2900 Crystal Drive, Arlington, VA 22202-3513. You can also pay by credit card using a form on the PTO Web site.

Stage 3: Making it through the application review process

In this phase of the process, a PTO examiner checks over your application more carefully and makes a decision as to whether your domain name may be registered. There are several "substantive" reasons for which an examiner may reject a trademark application. These commonly include marks that:

- ✔ Consist of or comprise immoral, deceptive, or scandalous matter.

- ✔ Disparage or falsely suggest a connection with persons (living or dead), institutions, beliefs, or national symbols, or bring them into contempt or disrepute.

- ✔ Consist of or comprise a name identifying a particular living individual (except by that individual's written consent) or the name of a deceased President of the United States during the life of his widow, if any, except by the written consent of the widow.

- ✔ So resemble a mark already registered in the Patent and Trademark Office (PTO) that use of the mark on the applicant's goods or services are likely to cause confusion, mistake, or deception.

*Consist of a generic, merely descriptive mark.

If the PTO examiner decides that your mark cannot be registered — or that your application requires some corrections — he or she will contact you and explain the situation. If you want to respond to the objections, you must do so within six months or forfeit your application by appealing to the PTO Trademark Trial and Appeal Board (TTAB).

There is no appeal after the initial six month period. If you fail to respond to an examiner's inquiry or refusal, your application will be considered abandoned. If, however, you do respond within the six month period and the examiner makes the refusal or inquiry final, only then can you seek appeal to the TTAB.

If your application meets all the examiner's objections, it moves forward into the next stage of the registration process.

Stage 4: Notice and opposition

In this stage, your registration application is published in the PTO's weekly *Official Gazette*. Anyone who opposes the trademark registration of your mark may do so within 30 days from the publication date.

If an opposition to the registration of your mark is filed, the PTO Trademark Trial and Appeal Board will hold an opposition proceeding. If no one opposes the registration of your mark, it proceeds to the next stage in the process.

Stage 5: Approval of your federal trademark registration

At this stage, you and your trademark are home free. Here is what you can expect about six months from the date of publication, provided that no opposition, or notice of opposition, is filed within the first 30 days:

✔ **If your application was based on the actual use of your mark in commerce, the PTO will register the mark and issue a registration certificate.**

✔ **If your application was based on the *intent* to use your mark in commerce, the PTO will issue a "Notice of Allowance."** You then have six months from the date of the notice to either:

  • Use the mark in commerce and submit a "Statement of Use" For $100

  • Request a six-month "Extension of Time to File a Statement of Use" for a fee of $150

When you file your "Statement of Use" and the PTO approves it, you are then issued your trademark registration certificate.

Getting Additional Help When You Need It

After you submit your trademark application, you can check on its status in one of two ways:

✔ Call the PTO status line at 703-305-8747 (have your serial number and/or registration number handy when you call).

✔ Go to the PTO's Trademark Applications and Registrations Retrieval (TARR) database at `tarr.uspto.gov`.

For other trademark assistance, turn to these resources:

✔ General Trademark or Patent Information: 703-308-4357

✔ Automated (Recorded) General Trademark or Patent Information: 703-557-4636

✔ Assignment & Certification Branch (Assignments, Changes of Name, and Certified Copies of Applications and Registrations): 703-308-9723

✔ Trademark Assistance Center: 703-308-9000

✔ Information Regarding Renewals, Affidavits of Use, Incontestability, or Correcting a Mistake on a Registration: 703-308-9500

✔ Information Regarding Applications Based on International Agreements or for Certification, Collective, or Collective Membership Marks: 703-308-9000

✔ Trademark Trial and Appeal Board: 703-308-9300

✔ Assistant Commissioner for Trademarks: 703-308-8900

You can also turn to the following resources for useful information on trademarks:

✔ **International Trademark Association (INTA).** 1133 Avenue of the Americas, New York, NY 10036; phone: 212-768-9887; fax: 212-768-7796; Web site: `www.inta.org`

✔ **Local Patent and Trademark Depository Libraries.** For a listing of the libraries, go to `www.uspto.gov/web/offices/ac/ido/ptdl/ptdlib_1.html`

✔ **The Sunnyvale Center on Innovation, Invention, and Ideas.** 465 South Mathilda Avenue, Suite 300, Sunnyvale, CA 94086; phone: 408-730-7290; Web site: `www.sci3.com`

Using an attorney

The trademark application process is straightforward enough that an attorney's help is rarely if ever required. Nevertheless, consultation with an experienced attorney or other professional may save you the time-consuming trouble of fixing problems with your application down the road. A trademark lawyer's expertise and assistance is especially valuable, however, if the PTO rejects your trademark for one of the "substantive" reasons and you want to challenge that ruling. On the other hand, an experienced attorney may be able to draft the application in a manner that will reduce the likelihood that an examiner will initially reject the application.

If you want to enlist the help of a trademark attorney, you can find listings of them in your local Yellow Pages and through your local bar association.

Using a trademark firm

If you do not want to go through the process of preparing and submitting a trademark application yourself, you have the option of using the services of a trademark firm. A number of these companies will assist you with preparing your application and submitting it for federal trademark registration, for a price around $300, including a comprehensive trademark search (the PTO application filing fee is extra).

Firms that offer federal trademark registrations services include:

- ✔ **4TradeMark.com,** 1000 West Avenue, Suite 1114, Miami Beach, FL 33139; phone: 800-4-TRADEMARK; Web site: 4trademark.com.

- ✔ **NameProtect,** Web site: www.nameprotect.com. NameProtect offers a user-friendly AutoMark online trademark application tool for $65 (plus the PTO filing fee), as well as filing assistance provided by attorneys.

- ✔ **Trademark Center,** 21550 Oxnard Street, Suite 300, Woodland Hills, CA 91367; phone: 800-705-9600 (toll-free); Web site: www.tmcenter.com

- ✔ **Trademark Express,** with offices in California and Washington, D.C.:

  Northern California office: 4546 El Camino Real, Suite 250, Los Altos, CA 94022; phone: 800-776-0530 or 650-948-0530; Web site: www.trademarkexpress.com/

  Southern California office: Harbor Boulevard, Suite 202, Costa Mesa, CA 92626; phone: 800-550-1520 (toll-free) or 714-437-1520; Web site: www.trademarkexpress.com

  Washington D.C, office: 1901 Pennsylvania Avenue NW, Suite 900, Washington DC, 20006; phone: 800-340-2010 or 202-496-1600; Web site: www.trademarkexpress.com

---

Applying for a U.S. trademark when you don't live in the U.S.

If you are not a U.S. citizen and would like to apply for United States federal trademark registration, you may do so, using an agent in the U.S., in the following situations:

- ✔ You use your mark in interstate commerce or commerce between the United States and a foreign country.

- ✔ You have the bona fide or good faith intention to use the mark in interstate commerce

or commerce between the United States and a foreign country.

- ✔ You have filed a trademark application in a foreign country within the last six months.

- ✔ You own a foreign trademark registration and have a certified copy.

Getting an International Trademark

Obtaining federal trademark registration only protects your domain name within the confines of the United States and its territories. However, if you have a U.S. federal trademark, a competing trademark holder in another country will have a much more difficult time taking your domain name away from you or prohibiting you from using it.

If you want to strengthen your domain name's protections in other countries in which you do business, look into applying for trademark registrations in each of those foreign countries in which you do business or use your mark. Or consider international registration through the World Intellectual Property Organization (WIPO). You can get information about international trademark application procedures from WIPO at `www.wipo.org/activities/en` or from the International Trademark Association (INTA) at `www.inta.org`.

Protecting Your Trademark

One additional step you can take to protect trademark rights that attach to your domain name is to use the services of a *trademark monitoring firm*. These companies notify you of domain names and applications to register trademarks that could be confusingly similar to your mark, thus alerting you to potential infringement issues.

Companies that provide these monitoring services include

- ✔ **Cyveillance** (`www.cyveillance.com`), offering fee-based monthly intellectual property protection reporting.

- ✔ **NameProtect** (`www.nameprotect.com`), offering free NameGuard monthly Watch Reports on potential threats to your domain name.

- ✔ **Trademark Express** (`www.trademarkexpress.com`), providing research on conflicting and similar marks.

If someone is infringing on your trademark . . .

As soon as you discover that someone may be violating your trademark rights, the best thing to do is to contact a trademark attorney. The lawyer will help you draft and send the potentially offending party a letter declaring that you hold trademark rights and putting him or her on notice not to infringe those rights. The earlier you put someone on notice in this manner, the stronger you chances will be of averting or successfully ending a dispute.

If you are infringing on someone else's trademark . . .

If you receive a letter from a trademark holder warning you about potential infringement, seek the help of an experienced trademark attorney, who can provide you with appropriate legal advice.

Part IV
Buying a Domain Name

The 5th Wave   By Rich Tennant

"I'm sorry, but 'Arf', 'Bark', and 'Woof' are already registered domain names. How about 'Oink', 'Quack', or 'Moo'?"

In this part . . .

*I*f the domain name you want has already been taken by someone else, you're not without hope. Buying the domain name you're looking for is a great alternative. But just as when you buy anything else of value, you need to do a little legwork first, and in this part, we show you how. You'll find useful information on the domain name resale market, which will make the buying process go much more smoothly for you. And we let you know how you can be sure (or at least more certain) about how much the domain name you're after is really worth.

Chapter 9

Buying a Domain Name on the Resale Market

. . . .

In This Chapter

▶ Going directly through the current owner to buy a domain name

▶ Understanding the process of buying a previously owned domain name

▶ Working with a domain name broker

▶ Buying a domain name from an auction site

. . . .

*E*ven if the domain name you want has been registered by someone else, you may still be able to acquire it — or a good alternative — on the increasingly active domain name resale market. Although the price will likely be considerably more than a domain name registration fee, it may well be worth the extra cost to you if you need a great domain name for your business.

Sales of previously registered domain names are flourishing as the supply of top-quality, unregistered domain names dwindles. As with the real estate market, prices for Internet addresses fluctuate. The good news for buyers is that the recent frenzy of domain name pricing has tapered off, and the average sale price has been coming down. The high end can range from $100,000 to $1 million, but most domain names sell for a much more reasonable amount, around $3,000 per name. What will happen to domain name prices in the future, however, is anyone's guess, especially with ICANN's approval of the new TLDs. Nevertheless, if you want a great domain name for your business, and you have not been able to find an unregistered name that works well for you, there is an excellent chance that you can acquire one that has been previously owned.

In this chapter, we look at different approaches you can take to purchasing a name, from directly contacting the owner to working with a domain name broker or an auction site. We share tips, discuss the pros and cons, and give you the inside information you need to make a good deal on the best possible domain name.

Buying a Domain Name Directly from the Owner

The most direct way to buy a domain name on the resale market is to contact the owner of that name and make a purchase offer. The contact for every domain name registration is readily available, so if you know the name you want, you can easily figure out who owns it.

Caution: Contacting the owner may be the most direct way to buy a name, but it is also the riskiest. If you do not use a professional intermediary, such as a broker or escrow service, you will have less information about the owner and less control over contract and payment issues (later in this chapter we discuss how to work with brokers and escrow companies).

Using whois to find the owner

The whois database (covered in more detail in Chapter 5) is the key to discovering the identity of a domain name's owner. Here how you can put whois to work for you:

1. **Go to the whois tool on the Web site of a domain name registrar, such as register.com.**

2. **Type in the domain name whose owner you're looking for.**

   A screen appears telling you that the domain name has already been registered.

3. **Click on the domain name to find out who registered it.**

   A screen appears detailing the contact information for the domain name owner.

So, for example, if you're just dying to buy the domain name Amazon.com, you can follow these steps to find out who the registered owner of the domain name is. And Figure 9-1 shows the contact information you would find.

After you have this information, you may want to browse the Web to see if the owner is actually using the domain name for a Web site. If not, there is a reasonable chance that the owner will be open to a purchase offer. (If you find that the domain name is being used for a huge online bookstore, however, you may want to consider other domain names instead.)

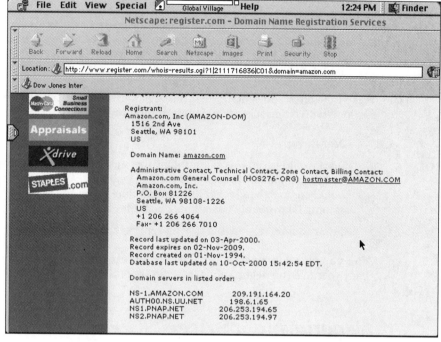

Screenshot courtesy of register.com

Figure 9-1:
You can use
the whois
database to
discover
who owns
the domain
name you're
interested in
buying.

Making an offer

After you've determined who owns the domain name you're interested in,
your next step is to contact the registration owner by e-mail and make an initial offer to buy the name. For this first contact, don't disclose many details
about your business or even your location, because the seller may interpret
that information as a reason to inflate his asking price.

For example, if you reveal to the owner that you are starting a well-funded
financial venture in Manhattan, the owner would have higher price expectations than if you were starting a small home business in Des Moines. No
matter what business you are engaged in or where you are located, keep your
cards close to your vest at this stage in the process.

Come up with a price range of how much you would be willing to spend — for
example, $5,000 to $7,500 — but don't actually name a figure in your e-mail.
Put the onus on the seller to set the price.

Your e-mail should set the tone of your negotiations. Here is an example of an
opening round e-mail that you may send to a domain name registration
holder:

Dear Owner,

I am thinking of starting a business. I came across your domain name and thought it may work for my venture. If you have a reasonable expectation in terms of a sales price, I may consider making you an offer. I don't have too much to spend, but I would be interested in your response.

Some time after you send off that initial email, the potential seller may respond with a message that sounds something like this:

Dear Buyer,

Yes, I would be interested in selling, because I am not doing anything with that domain name. I registered it three years ago and thought that it would come in handy, but I never had time to get the venture off the ground. I'd probably consider selling it for $25,000 to $30,000.

If that sounds reasonable to you, send me an e-mail.

After you pick yourself up off the floor and recover from price shock, you are ready to move the negotiations into the second phase — negotiating a price.

Negotiating a price

When you get a reply from the domain name's owner, you can probably tell whether he actually needs the domain name himself. In the example in the preceding section, you can tell that the owner doesn't really need the domain name, but he also doesn't need to sell it. As a result, he is not highly motivated to make a deal.

To continue the negotiation and bring it more in line with your budget expectations, you could respond this way:

Dear Seller,

Thanks for your reply. The $25,000 to $30,000 price is beyond my range. I was actually thinking that $3,000 to $5,000 would be more in line.

Keep in mind that if you offer $3,000 to $5,000, you are in fact making an offer of $5,000, because no seller will opt for the lower figure.

Here is the type of response that you may receive from the seller:

Dear Buyer,

I really appreciate your offer. I understand that your money's on the line and that your venture is not likely to be a huge profit maker. As a compromise, why we don't we try $10,000 to $12,500. If you can pay it all in cash within two weeks, we just may have a deal.

At this point, if you really want the name, you may consider responding with a counteroffer something like this:

> Dear Seller,
>
> I've thought about it. I'm going to dig deep and make you an offer of $7,500, payable in seven days, and I'll pay all the expediting fees. What do you say?

Don't forget that patience is essential during a negotiation. If you frequently e-mail and pester the domain name owner to make a decision, any reasonably shrewd seller will realize that you are a motivated buyer, and the price will go up as a result. If you rush someone into a decision, either the deal will collapse or you will pay a premium. Give each other ample time to contemplate the deal without feeling rushed.

If all goes well, you may get an e-mail from the seller that looks something like this:

> Dear Buyer,
>
> You have a deal.

Congratulations! You are now close to possessing the domain name that you really want. But the deal is not closed yet. Like buying a house, you still have to jump many hurdles before you actually own the name.

Working out the kinks

The next step is working out with the seller any contingencies you both may require, such as trademark searches or any loan requirements. When those have been negotiated, you and the seller are ready to close the deal.

Blue-light special: Expired domain names

Repossessed domain names are names whose original registrations have expired because their owners failed to pay the renewal fee on time — or at all. When that happens, the names return to the pool of unregistered domain names, and anyone can pick them up for the low-cost registration fee.

Every week, thousands of domain names expire. For a fee, you can subscribe to a list that will regularly inform you of all the latest repossessed monikers on the market. Two of these subscription services are:

✔ **DNS Research** (www.dnsresearch.com)

✔ **Unclaimed Domains** (www.unclaimed-domains.com)

Advice your mother would give

Your mom may or may not be hip to the Internet Age, but even if she isn't yet cruising the Information Superhighway, here are a few suggestions that she would surely approve of (and we all know that mothers know best, right?):

✔ **Don't forget to do a trademark search on a domain name before you buy it.** A number of domain name resellers provide links from their site directly to services such as NameProtect, so that you can quickly and easily check out a name before you put your money on the line.

✔ **Patience is a virtue.** Your new domain name is not really yours until you have the final paperwork. As a result, you can't use or publicize your new Internet address in any way — whether in printing new business stationery or brochures, purchasing ads, or issuing press releases — until the name is actually and entirely in your possession.

If you have contingencies, make sure to get the seller's agreement before you take the next step. If you spring any surprises at that point, you could blow the deal.

Closing the deal

To begin the closing phase, you and the seller should exchange confirmation e-mails with one another, detailing all the points and terms of the agreement. E-mails *may* be legally enforceable, but typically they serve as an agreement to agree. Just like you would not put a down payment on a house based on an exchange of e-mails, you should not pay any money to the seller at this point. The deal can still fall apart for a variety of reasons.

The best thing you can do to make the deal legal (and safe) for both you and the seller is to bring in the services of an escrow company — a neutral third party — to conclude the deal. The following section covers escrow services in greater detail.

Transferring a domain name's registration

When you buy a domain name from a previous owner, the registration must be transferred to you before the sale can be completed. The remainder of the current owner's registration term will be transferred to the domain name's buyer once the process has been completed.

To legally transfer the domain name, the seller must complete the Registrant Name Change Agreement (RNCA). Many registrars provide this service, although not all of them do. Some registrars provide transfer service at no cost, whereas others charge a $35 fee for the service.

The standard processing time usually takes three to six weeks. Network Solutions, however, can complete the transfer in as little as two days, after the buyer and seller provide all the required information. The charge for this expedited service is $199, an expense that is usually invoiced to the buyer.

Only the actual registration holder for the domain name can authorize a Registrant Name Change Agreement. If, during the escrow process, it becomes apparent that the seller is not the true registered owner of the name, the sale will be cancelled.

To complete the registration transfer, the buyer and seller must typically provide the following information:

- ✔ **Notarized letter authorizing the transfer, provided by the current registration holder.**

- ✔ **Complete contact and billing information, if necessary, for the current registrant.**

- ✔ **Complete contact and billing information, if necessary, for the new registrant, whether the buyer is an individual or the administrative contact for a business.**

- ✔ **A Transfer of Registrant Agreement, signed and dated by both the current and new domain name registrants.**

- ✔ **A Registration Agreement signed by the new registrant.**

Working with an Escrow Company

Escrow is a piece of property held in trust by an impartial third party. Working with an escrow company reduces the chances of fraud and ensures the safety of a transaction from the perspective of both the buyer and the seller. Most homebuyers and sellers use escrow companies to facilitate the transfer of property, and using an escrow service for a domain name sale can be very wise as well, especially for purchases above $1,000.

As a buyer, using an escrow service gives you the security of knowing that you will actually receive the domain name registration you are purchasing after you pay the contracted price.

You can use any one of a number of online escrow services. GreatDomains.com's escrow service (at www.greatdomains.com) specializes in domain name transactions. Other escrow sites include:

- ✔ **Escrow.com** (www.escrow.com)
- ✔ **Tradenable** (www.tradenable.com)

For purchases above $100, fees range from 1 percent to 4 percent of the sales price. The escrow fee may be paid either by the buyer or the seller — this is something that you and the seller of the domain name can negotiate.

With GreatDomains.com, the escrow process works like this:

1. **You and the seller provide all pertinent information to the escrow company.**

2. **A verification e-mail is sent to you and the seller.**

3. **When the escrow company receives the verification from both parties, the transfer process is initiated.**

4. **The escrow company sends the Purchase Agreement, Escrow Agreement, transfer documents, and payment instructions to you (the buyer).**

5. **You have five business days to complete and return the documents and fund the transaction.**

6. **At the same time, the escrow company verifies through whois that the seller actually has rights to the registration of the domain name.**

    The transaction is contingent upon successful verification from the registrar.

7. **When the escrow company receives all the documentation from you, they send all required documents to the seller.**

8. **The seller has three business days to complete and return the documents to the escrow company.**

9. **When the escrow service has confirmed with the registrar that the transfer is successful, it remits the requisite funds to the seller, minus the escrow fee.**

The full transfer process can take approximately three weeks. Both the buyer and the seller must complete and return the documents within the required time frame or risk having the process canceled. Of course, this process may differ substantially from one transaction to another, or between different providers of escrow services.

"For sale by owner" Web sites

If you want to buy a domain name directly from its owner, you can also work through a "for sale by owner" Web site. These sites carry listings of domain names for sale, often with no associated brokerage fees or commissions. More than a dozen of these sites are in existence, including:

✔ **ABCOM Domain Name Resales** (www. fastprofits.net)

✔ **AllFreeDomains.com** (www. allfreedomains. com)

✔ **ComBuys.com** (www.combuys.com)

✔ **DomainBook.com** (www.domainbook. com)

✔ **eDomainRealty.com** (www. edomainrealty. com)

✔ **URLResources.com** (www.urlresources. com)

Using a Domain Name Broker

If you would rather not deal directly with a potential seller, another, advantageous, alternative is to purchase a name through a *domain name broker*. Like real estate brokers, domain name brokers are specialists in the Internet real estate market. They deal with thousands of domain name transactions every year. Domain name brokers have the experience and business relationships not only to bring buyers and sellers together successfully but also to smooth the resale purchasing and selling experience.

A broker can work with you as an Internet real estate expert to:

✔ Find a domain name that is right for you or your business.

✔ Oversee the negotiating process, with buyers and sellers remaining anonymous to each other.

✔ Facilitate the closing of the deal, including escrow and domain name transfer arrangements.

All of this can work to your advantage as the buyer, especially because the seller of the domain name usually pays the broker's commission (usually around 15 percent). Many domain name brokers are on the Internet, including:

✔ **The Domain Emporium** (www.thedomainemporium.com)

✔ **DomainRealtor.com** (www.domainrealtor.com)

✔ **GreatDomains.com** (www.greatdomains.com)

✔ **Time2Sell** (www.time2sell.com)

The buying strategy provided by many brokers is called the *negotiated offer process*. It has a lot in common with the real estate purchasing process in that the buyer makes an offer on a listing, the seller accepts or counteroffers, the deal is brought to closing, and the property changes hands — all through the intermediary of the broker, who serves as a buffer between the buyer and the seller.

The difference with the negotiated offer process in the domain name secondary market is that almost the *entire* transaction takes place online, and it can be accomplished in as little as three days. Many brokers offer domain name listings and facilitate the negotiated offer process.

GreatDomains.com has been a pioneer in this domain name purchasing approach. To explore what is involved, here's a step-by-step look at its negotiated offer procedure:

1. **Go to `www.greatdomains.com` and click on "New Users Join Now."**

   The registration screen appears.

2. **Fill in your contact information, and select a logon name and password.**

3. **Read the User Agreement, and then click "Create Account."**

   The Welcome to GreatDomains.com screen appears.

4. **Click on Buy a Domain.**

5. **Use the search tool to find a list of domain names that have the qualities you want.**

   For example, if you want to see domain names that would be appropriate for a sports equipment business, you could start by typing "sports" into the search bar. In the case of "sports," for example, over 14,000 available names are listed.

6. **Narrow your search.**

   Choosing a particular extension limits the choice, but you may still end up with more domain names than you can possibly review. Limit the field further by narrowing the listing to those that are within the price range you want.

To a great extent, with domain names, you get what you pay for. Although there may in fact be suitable names available at a price under $1,000, the best names typically cost more. Think about why you need the name, how much your business will depend on it, and consider carefully how much of an investment you should make.

7. If you find a name you like, click on the name to get to the Details page for that particular name.

This page provides a description of good potential uses for the name, displays the asking price, and includes a box in which you can type in an offer.

8. If you want to take the process further, make an offer.

A good strategy, generally speaking, is to start by offering 70 percent to 80 percent of the price you are willing to pay.

If you make an offer that is above the minimum bid for that particular name, you arrive at the offer confirmation page.

9. Confirm your offer.

You will receive an e-mail verifying your offer. After you verify the offer amount, it will be submitted, and the negotiating process will start.

You can view the progress of your offer at any time by going to "My Account" and clicking on "My Offers." You can cancel an offer at any time until the seller responds. After the seller has responded, however, your offer is binding.

10. Negotiate a price.

Within 72 hours, GreatDomains.com will notify you by e-mail whether your offer has been accepted, declined, or countered. If it has been countered, you have the opportunity to accept the counteroffer or counter once again. For example, if the domain name you want is listed with the asking price of $2,000, and you make an initial offer of $1,500, the seller may counter with $1,900. You may decline the counter, accept it, or counteroffer again — with, for example, an offer of $1,750.

Look to see how much movement you are getting from the seller. If she keeps making higher counteroffers, she may not be motivated to sell. A motivated seller is more likely to move toward a compromise. For example, if you offer $5,000 for a name and the seller counters at $10,000, if she is motivated, she may agree to sell at a price between $6,000 and $8,000.

11. Close the deal.

If your offer is accepted, you will be notified of the good news by e-mail, informing you that an escrow representative will contact you to take you through the escrow and domain name transfer process. At this point, you are in a binding contract to purchase the name. In many cases, the entire negotiated offer process can be completed in one day, or there may be as many as six to eight counteroffers over a three-day period.

Just as with buying a house, many things can still go wrong during the escrow process before the deal is finalized. The main thing to remember is that the domain name is not yours until it has actually been transferred to your name.

Going the fixed price route

In addition to the negotiated offer process, you also have the option of purchasing a domain name at a fixed price through a new service offered by GreatDomains.com. This approach avoids the often time-consuming and uncertain back-and-forth of price negotiations.

In the fixed-price purchase model, the seller places a specific price tag on the name. If the domain name meets your business and budget requirements, you simply buy the name at that price, and the entire purchase process is completed quickly. In many cases, the purchase can be paid for immediately by credit card, speeding the conclusion of the deal.

Bidding on a Domain Name through an Auction Site

If you don't want to buy a domain name directly from the owner or work with a domain name broker, another alternative is to use one of the online auction sites that carries listings of domain names, such as eBay (`www.ebay.com`), Yahoo! (`auctions.yahoo.com`), or Afternic (`www.afternic.com`).

Although auctions can be an effective way to buy many types of items, the auction model is only really effective where there is enough interest to generate competitive bids from at least two potential buyers. Unfortunately, when it comes to domain names, the vast majority never attract more than one bid. Nevertheless, for some higher-profile names — especially short, generic domain names that attract a lot of interest — auctions can work very well.

Auctions may not be the best way to buy a domain name if you're in a hurry to obtain one. Auction lengths may range from 24 hours to as long as 30 days, and you have no guarantee that you will actually obtain the name. If you're pressed for time, a negotiated sale or a fixed-price purchase (covered earlier in the chapter) is a better option for you.

Understanding the auction process

Although each auction site has its own specific rules and procedures, the following steps are generally consistent from site to site:

1. **Go to the auction Web site.**

   Domain name auctions are held at:

- **Afternic** (www.afternic.com)

- **ChoiceFree** (www.choicefree.com)

- **TheDomainAuction.com** (www.thedomainauction.com)

- **eBay** (www.ebay.com, or go to listings.ebay.com/aw/listings/list/all/category3767 for domain name listings).

- **NamesForBid.com** (www.namesforbid.com)

- **Shoutloud.com** (www.shoutloud.com)

- **SolutionHome.com** (www.solutionhome.com/auction.htm)

- **Yahoo! Auctions** (auctions.yahoo.com, or go directly to auctions.yahoo.com/27751-category-leaf.html for domain name listings)

2. **Register or join the auction site as a user.**

   In most cases, registering entails providing your e-mail address, reading and accepting a user service agreement, entering your credit card information, and confirming your e-mail address, a user name, and a password of your choice.

3. **Pay a fee, if necessary.**

   Some sites may charge a small fee to complete the registration process.

4. **Search the site for a domain name that you want to bid on.**

   Go to the Auctions page and scroll the category list or use the search function to generate a list of available domain names that interest you, such as business, sports, or travel. Keep in mind that prices vary widely, from $15 to $3 million or more.

5. **Put a bid on that name.**

   When you find a domain name that you want, simply click on it and enter a bid. If someone outbids you, the auction site will notify you by e-mail.

Once you make and confirm a bid, you are legally bound to pay that amount if the seller accepts your offer. Make sure you really want the domain name and are prepared to pay the price that you bid.

Most auction rules have several types of bidding features, including the following:

  ✔ **Starting bid:** This is the minimum amount that anyone can offer when a domain name auction starts.

  ✔ **Minimum bid:** After the first bid has been made, this is the next acceptable bid. The figure is based on the previous bid plus a certain set increment.

✔ **Reserve price:** This is usually higher than the starting bid, and it is the lowest bid that the seller will accept. If bidding does not reach the reserve price, the domain name will not be sold. For example, a seller may set the starting bid for a domain name at $300 and a reserve price at $3,000. If bidding does not reach $3,000, the domain name will not be sold. Sellers often, however, name a low reserve price to generate interest in the auction, hoping that competitive bidding will drive the price above that threshold.

✔ **Buy price:** If a seller specifies a buy price, he or she will sell the domain name immediately after a bid at that level has been made. The seller can also choose to sell below that buy price if he or she so chooses.

✔ **Automatic or proxy bidding:** This feature enables you to continue bidding on a domain name even after you have left the Auction site. To place these bids, simply indicate the maximum amount that you are willing to pay. The system will automatically enter bids on your behalf, at the lowest possible increment, until the auction is over or you have reached your maximum.

Knowing what to do if you win

If the seller accepts your bid, the auction site will notify you by e-mail. You and the seller should then move into the escrow process (covered earlier in this chapter) and the transfer of the domain name registration.

TIP

Do I hear $950?: The rules of the road for auctions

To make sure your auction purchasing experience is as safe and positive as possible, follow these rules of the road:

✔ **Keep copies of all documentation.** Print out and retain electronic records of all bids, agreements, payments, and other auction information. The auction sites will not provide these documents for you.

✔ **Check the domain name registration before you bid.** Before you make a purchase offer on a domain name, use whois to check out whether the name really belongs to the person who is offering it for sale.

✔ **Do some trademark research before you make an offer.** If you are serious about the name, and if it requires a substantial

investment, do some trademark research on it to make sure that it is a safe name to use before you make your bid.

✔ **Get the name appraised before you buy it.** This is particularly advisable for domain names costing over $1,000. You can get a basic sense of a name's value on the market by using the valuation model in Chapter 10. You can also obtain appraisal services at sites like Domain IQ (www.domainiq.com/appraisals.htm), GreatDomains.com (www.greatdomains.com/services/appraisal/appraisalinfo.asp), or SolutionHome.com (www.solutionhome.com/appraisal).

Some sites provide online tools to facilitate the paperwork involved.

Making the payment

Although some auction sites accept credit card payments, others only accept one of the following:

- ✔ **Wire transfers:** A payment you authorize your bank to make directly to another bank.

- ✔ **Cashier's checks:** Payments issued by the bank and prepaid by you.

- ✔ **Money orders:** Prepaid checks that you can purchase at the U.S. Post Office branches, banks, Western Union, and other service companies.

- ✔ **An online payment service:** Services such as Yahoo! PayDirect or PayPal, which enable you to send money online from an account funded by your credit card or checking account.

Domain name sales under $100,000

Although sales of domain names have reached the figure of $7.5 million, most names sell for considerably less. To give you an idea of the quality of names that have been purchased at resale on the market, here is a list of 20 names that have sold for less than $100,000 (for a list of the top ten prices paid for domain names, turn to Chapter 17):

- ✔ **Perfect.com:** $94,000
- ✔ **Trade.com:** $94,000
- ✔ **InternetBank.com:** $92,800
- ✔ **Birdie.com:** $90,000
- ✔ **Counselors.com:** $85,000

- ✔ **Culture.com:** $69,325
- ✔ **IBC.com:** $60,770
- ✔ **HappyBirthday.com:** $55,000
- ✔ **Net-Broker.com:** $52,500
- ✔ **CarNet.com:** $50,000
- ✔ **Domestic Films.com:** $50,000
- ✔ **ShoppingMall.com:** $50,000
- ✔ **1ClickLenders.com:** $45,000
- ✔ **Foto.com:** $45,000
- ✔ **Receivables.com:** $40,000

Chapter 10

Valuing a Domain Name

. . . .

. . . .

Setting the right price for a domain name — and offering a fair price to buy one — is essential for anyone who wants to win in the domain name market. But when price tags for some premium names have been jumping from $100,000 to $3 million in just one year, the process of accurately valuing a domain name can seem baffling, if not downright impossible.

That's where this chapter can help you navigate your way through the often rough waters of the domain name market. Here you get the lowdown on why the value of your domain name, or one you're considering buying, is important. Then you use GreatDomains.com's proprietary four C valuation method (no, we're not talking diamonds here) to determine the value of a domain name. With this approach, you can be fairly confident that you know a domain name's value — and you won't pay more for it (or sell it for less) than it's worth.

Note: References to these proprietary methodologies should not be construed as a license to use, make or sell products or services that may be covered under these proprietary methodologies. The consent of GreatDomains. com should be obtained prior to any commercial use thereof.

Understanding the Importance of a Domain Name's Value

Ignorance may be bliss when it comes to some things in life, but definitely not when it comes to domain names. Assessing the value of any domain name that you want to sell or buy is vital for several reasons. If you're a seller and you price your name too high, you may have to wait months or even years for the market to catch up to your demands. Although you may be tempted, in a rising market, to ask extraordinarily high prices for domain name property, unrealistic price tags can actually discourage bids and make your domain name almost impossible to sell. Unless you're in absolutely no hurry to make a deal, determining the true value of your domain name and pricing it according to the market pays off.

On the other hand, if you ask too little for a domain name, you could miss out on considerable sales profits. Many people make the mistake of underpricing if they're in a rush to sell or if they haven't taken the time to educate themselves about the domain name marketplace. Either way, if you overprice or under-price a name, you're losing money you could be using to line your pocket.

Not knowing the real value of a domain name can be just as hazardous for people looking to buy. For example, the practice of lowballing or under bidding — a common tactic in business negotiations — can backfire in the domain name marketplace. Many sellers are insulted by such low offers, and they may even exclude lowballers from future bidding opportunities. At the very least, underbidders risk losing the domain name to a competitor who more clearly understands its value and marketing potential and bids accordingly.

Overbidding can also be a problem for domain name buyers. No buyer wants to overpay for a domain name, but over the long haul, this error may be less cause for concern than underbidding. As Marc Ostrofsky proved when he bought the domain name Business.com for what seemed like a very hefty $150,000 but then sold it two years later for $7.5 million, the rise in domain name values may turn what once seemed like a foolhardy purchase into a shrewd investment.

Knowing the Four Cs of Domain Names

Fortunately, valuing a domain name is more scientific than simple trial and error, relying on your gut instinct, or sticking a finger in the wind. As with any asset, understanding the underlying factors that determine a domain name's value is important. Diamonds, for example, are evaluated according to their rating on the four Cs: cut, color, clarity, and carat weight. Domain names, too, can be assessed according to their rating on a different but equally important set of four Cs — characters, commerce, .com, and comps — covered in the following sections.

Characters

The first of the four Cs — *characters* — refers to a domain name's length. A basic rule when it comes to the Internet is that briefer is almost always better. From the time it takes to download a Web page to the length of a paragraph displayed on the screen, brevity and speed count for a lot in this fast-paced world. Internet users, as a group, do not have much patience. Most would rather click on another site than put up with any cumbersome, time-wasting process.

This rule holds true with domain names. After all, most people have to type a domain name into their browser bar to reach the site they want. The longer the domain name, the more of a hassle it is to remember, and the greater the chances that the person will make a spelling or typing error. In the abbreviated world of the Internet, a short, memorable domain name such as xyz.com is much more valuable than jklmnopqrstuvwxyz.com, for obvious reasons.

Short domain names are also more valuable than long ones because they're rarer. For example, only 676 combinations of two-letter domain names exist and only 17,576 combinations of three-letter names. The number increases exponentially the longer the name. Like prime beachfront property, short domain names are in limited supply, which drives up their value. And, like choice real estate, a certain level of prestige is associated with short names, and that prestige increases their value even more. Because people know short names are rare and hard to acquire, they can command a premium price.

Commerce

The second C stands for *commerce*. From a pricing standpoint, having a name that can easily be applied to online business is a clear advantage. More than any other factor, the value of a domain name is driven by its ability to deliver traffic — and revenues — to a Web-based enterprise. The clearer that business connection, and the bigger the industry involved, the greater the value of the domain name.

.com

The third C stands for *.com*. In the domain name marketplace, the .com extension is simply more valuable than any other. The next most popular top-level domain — .net — is slowly gaining ground, but .net names are still only worth about 10 to 25 percent of .com names. Other gTLDs are even less valuable, selling for approximately 5 to 10 percent of the selling price of similar names with the .com suffix.

The popularity of .coms can be attributed to several factors. First, the .com extension usually designates business sites. If you're a commercial enterprise, but your domain name's extension is .net, .org, or something other than .com, your business may not be taken quite as seriously. Look at it this way: If top-level domains are the "location, location, location" of the virtual world, .com is the main business thoroughfare, and .net, .org, and other

TLDs are out-of-the-way side streets. Moreover, `.org` extensions are often associated with not-for-profit organizations, and `.net` TLDs are often linked to Internet Service Providers.

A second reason for the premium paid for .coms is that the phrase *dot-com* itself has turned into a synonym for *e-commerce* and *Internet-based enterprise.* Like the abbreviation *Inc.* after a corporate name, `.com`, to a certain extent at least, signifies a serious, purposeful, business presence on the Internet and an awareness of the e-commerce playing field.

Comps

The fourth C stands for *comps,* or sales of comparable property. In real estate, buyers and sellers rely on comps to determine the value of a home. To be useful, real estate comps should be similar to the property you're valuing in five basic categories: age, size, style, location, and condition. They should also be fairly recent — no more than six months old. To get a ballpark sense of a property's value, compare it to the selling price of at least three comps. The same method applies in valuing domain names. To get a realistic sense of a domain name's market value, compare it to recent sales of domain names with similar ratings in the first three of the four C categories.

Determining a Domain Name's Value Using the Four C Method

Now that you know what the four Cs stand for, you can use them to put a value on the domain name you're interested in. To determine a range of value for a domain name, follow these steps:

1. **Assign a score to the domain name according to the first C, characters.**

   If the domain name has 1 to 5 characters, give it 4 points. If the domain name has 6 to 10 characters, give it 3 points. If it has 11 to 15 characters, give it 2 points. If it has 16 to 20 characters, give it 1 point. And if it has 21 or more characters, give it 0 points. To give you some examples, Amazon.com has 6 characters (you don't count the .com in the domain name), giving it a 3-point rating. Loans.com has 5 characters, giving it 4 points, and eBay.com has 4 characters, also giving it a 4-point score.

2. **Rate the domain name's commercial qualities using six different criteria.**

   To assess a name's commercial qualities, rate it on a scale of 1 to 4 (4 being the highest) on each of the following six criteria.

- **How obvious is the domain name's potential business use?** If you can easily see how a domain name could be used for business, that name is much more likely to attract potential bidders. For example, Cars.com is a more valuable domain name than Xx.com, because the potential business use for Cars.com is much more apparent than it is for Xx.com.

Companies with obscure domain names — imagine, for example, an online stock brokerage firm with the domain name Flightpath.com — have to spend millions of dollars trying to explain what business services they are offering to consumers. By contrast, a similar company with the domain name Stocks.com would have a fraction of the marketing expense, because consumers would automatically understand its services. The value of the domain name is directly related to the instant recognition and branding it can deliver for a business.

In addition to reducing marketing expense, a simple, generic, business-related domain name is especially valuable because it can automatically deliver visitors, or *traffic,* to a site. Every day, thousands of people looking for an online florist, for example, simply type Flowers.com into their browser bar. As a result, any business Web site that's linked to that name receives considerable traffic without any marketing or advertising at all — and, as any retailer knows, traffic is the most important key to sales.

- **How big is the related industry?** The greater the size of an industry, the higher the prices that related domain names can attract. Cars.com is more valuable than the domain name Fishingbait.com, for example, because the automobile industry is bigger than the fishing bait industry. Even though a name like Fishingbait.com may attract a lot of Internet traffic, it won't attract a premium sales price, because the potential revenues it can generate are relatively low.

You can determine the size of any industry you're interested in by searching the U.S. Department of Commerce Web site (www.doc. gov), checking industry association Web pages, reading trade magazines, and contacting related industry trade associations.

- **How well does the industry lend itself to e-commerce?** When it comes to doing business on the Internet, speed of product delivery is a top concern. Some businesses — such as those offering downloadable music — lend themselves extremely well to e-commerce, because they can instantly get their products into customers' hands. Other types of companies, such as online retailers, can deliver their goods in a matter of days. But some industries — office building construction, for example — don't have e-commerce applications that are as obvious. As a result, domain names related to those industries won't attract as high a price.

- **How rare or generic is the domain name?** Like the choicest property in exclusive neighborhoods, short, memorable, rare, and generic domain names command the highest prices. These names have instant branding potential and are the easiest for users to remember, spell, and type. Drugs.com, for example, is shorter, rarer, and simpler than Medications.com or Pharmaceuticals.com. Cars.com is more valuable than Automobiles.com, and Shoes.com is more valuable than Footwearunlimited.com. Because short, generic names are known to be so rare, they bestow instant cachet on the businesses that own them — a factor that increases their value even more.

  Generic domain names are also valuable because in many cases they can't be trademarked (see Chapter 6 for details). And in today's domain name marketplace, names with potential trademark issues are generally worthless because of the potential legal liabilities that accompany them. (See Chapter 5 for more information on domain name trademark issues.) As a firm rule, buyers should steer clear of domain names that could potentially infringe on the established trademark of any business or individual.

- **How many companies might want to buy the name?** Competitive bidding is the key to a high sales price. If an industry is large and growing, chances are that several companies will be interested in a prime, related domain name, and that drives up the name's value. Based on this criterion, for example, Baseballcaps.com will be a much more valuable domain name than Bowlerhats.com, unless bowlers hats start showing up on the fashion runways next season.

  To rate a domain name on this characteristic, research the relevant industry's growth and trends. How many businesses make up that industry? How many new companies are forming? Are revenue trends going up or down? The U.S. Department of Commerce and trade associations can be helpful sources of information.

- **How easily could the domain name be used as a brand name?** Simple, generic names can easily become brand names for online products or services. Domain names such as Music.com, Beer.com, or Books.com, for example, are all extremely *brandable,* meaning they're likely to catch on with consumers. Somewhat less valuable are variants of these names, such as Greatmusic.com, Brews.com, or Bookstore.com. Even less brandable variations would be Thousandsoftunes.com, Belgianbottledbeers.com, or Oldtravelbooks.com. And of course, CantTrustUs.com is an example of a domain name that probably has little branding potential, no matter what the business.

  Brandability can also relate to mental images and associations — qualities that can link a word to a product or service in the minds of customers. Amazon.com and Yahoo.com are successful examples of brands built around domain names. Unfortunately, however, given the huge growth in the number of online businesses, evocative but obscure domain names today require a huge outlay of advertising and marketing money to capture and keep customers' attention. As a result, they fetch a somewhat lower price than more obviously brandable domain names.

3. **Determine the domain name's** .com **rating. If the name has a** .com **TLD, assign it a 4. A** .net, .tv, **and** .cc **extension rates a 2. Any other TLD should be assigned a 1.**

4. **Here's where "comps" come in. Compare the score so far to sales of comparable domain names that have recently been sold.**

In real estate, buyers and sellers rely on *comps,* or sales of comparable property, to determine the value of a home. To be useful, real estate comps should be similar to the property you're valuing in five basic categories: age, size, style, location, and condition. They should also be fairly recent — no more than 6 months old. To get a ballpark sense of a property's value, compare it to the selling price of at least three comps.

The same method applies in valuing domain names. After you've scored a name on characters and commerce, compare it to recent sales of domain names with similar ratings. To find out the recent selling price of domain names, you can check newspaper reports and other published sources, as well as Web sites such as the *Domain Names For Dummies* Web site (www.greatdomains.com/dummies) or DomainNameNews.com (www.marksonline.com/locator/domnews.html), which provides news listings and reports on domain name record sales.

For a general range of domain name values based on prior sales of the domain names sold via GreatDomains.com, you can compare your domain name's score to the ratings in Table 10-1.

We know that Loans.com scores a 4 for characters and a 4 for commerce. According to Table 10-1, the approximate value ranges anywhere from $500,000 to $10 million, a very large price range. Knowing that the site's potential advertising value is $4 million over three years helps pinpoint a price. In fact, Loans.com sold in January 2000 to Bank of America for $3 million — a very reasonable purchase price, given its revenue potential.

Table 10-1	Domain Name Values				
Commerce Scores	**Characters Score 0**	**Characters Score 1**	**Characters Score 2**	**Characters Score 3**	**Characters Score 4**
Commerce Score 0	$0 to $10,000	$0 to $10,000	$0 to $10,000	$0 to $15,000	$0 to $20,000
Commerce Score 1	$0 to $15,000	$1,000 to $20,000	$3,000 to $25,000	$3,000 to $25,000	$5,000 to $50,000

(continued)

Table 10-1 *(continued)*

Commerce Scores	Characters Score 0	Characters Score 1	Characters Score 2	Characters Score 3	Characters Score 4
Commerce Score 2	$0 to $15,000	$1,000 to $40,000	$3,000 to $75,000	$5,000 to $100,000	$10,000 to $150,000
Commerce Score 3	$0 to $20,000	$5,000 to $50,000	$30,000 to $500,000	$50,000 to $1,000,000	$200,000 to $5,000,000
Commerce Score 4	$0 to $50,000	$10,000 to $250,000	$50,000 to $1,000,000	$300,000 to $5,000,000	$500,000 to $10,000,000

Adjust the valuation according to the domain name's extension.

If the domain name you're valuing is a .com, the approximate prices in Table 10-1 are a realistic range. If the domain name has a .net, .tv, or .cc extension, however, its value will be 10 to 25 percent of the prices given in the table. For all other extensions, the value will be approximately 5 to 10 percent of .com prices.

Another adjustment factor when you're determining the value of a domain name is timing. In a fast-rising domain name marketplace, names are more likely to sell for top dollar. In a slower market, however, when demand drops, names may take longer to sell and may go for lower prices. Whether you're a buyer or a seller, paying attention to trends and current sale prices in the domain name market is always important. Then you can plan your strategy accordingly.

Consulting an appraiser to get the value of your name

For a more precise valuation, you may want to consider paying for a professional appraisal. A number of Web sites, including GreatDomains.com, Domainappraiser.com, and Solutionhome.com, provide appraisal services, ranging in price from $20 to $100.

Depending on the appraiser's experience, and the size and quality of its database of comps, a professional assessment can give you a far more accurate and specific valuation than you would otherwise be able to obtain.

Part V

Profiting from Your Domain Name

THE MODERN JAMES BOND

The name is bond.com, JAMES bond.com.

In this part . . .

When you already have a domain name, you may be able to put that name to work for you by selling it, and in the chapters in this part, we show you how to do that. We also provide you with some fascinating and inspiring stories about people who've gotten creative by renting out their domain names for big bucks.

Chapter 11

Selling Your Domain Name

. . . .

In This Chapter

▶ Working with a domain name broker

▶ Knowing what to do when a buyer approaches you directly

▶ Listing your name as "for sale by owner"

▶ Using the negotiated offer process

▶ Selling your domain name at auction

. . . .

*A*ll the publicity about domain names selling for millions of dollars has sparked a wave of interest in the domain name secondary market — as well as high expectations on the part of many domain name holders. The fact is that the domain name resale market is thriving, but it is also true that most Internet addresses sell for far less that the highly publicized million-dollar domain name prices.

Just like in the physical, bricks-and-mortar real estate market, there is a wide range of values when it comes to Internet property. Some of these addresses sell quickly, at good prices, whereas the less marketable properties may be listed for a long time before they sell, if they sell at all. The average sale price during the first nine months of 2000, according to data gathered by GreatDomains.com, was $24,468, and the median sale price was $3,315.

Selling a domain name may not be the equivalent of cashing in a winning lottery ticket, but it can be a profitable activity — even in the lower price ranges. If you registered your domain name for $35 or $70 and you're not using it, you will realize a significant profit — with relatively little effort — if you sell it for even a few hundred dollars. That's a rate of return that's hard to beat.

In this chapter, we look at the different ways of selling domain names and how to increase your chances of a sale. You'll also find some great tips to keep in mind when you put your domain name on the market.

Considering Reasons to Sell

Selling a domain name can be an attractive option for individuals or businesses who registered Internet addresses that they have never developed into active Web sites. In many cases, the unused domain name may be an untapped asset worth far more on the resale market than you paid to register it. Good reasons for selling domain names include:

- **Unrealized plans.** Many people have registered domain names for Internet projects that they never got off the ground. If you have a good domain name that's just sitting on the shelf, you may be smart to convert that asset into cash.

- **Cyberinvesting.** For those who have always looked at domain names as financial investments, putting the right names up for sale — at the right time and for the right price — can be a winning move.

- **Unused assets.** Many companies — such as Procter & Gamble — have registered hundreds of premium domain names in case they wanted to use them for their own businesses down the road. If it becomes clear that those domain names will never be put to use, the most profitable strategy may be to list them for sale.

- **Offer to buy.** In many cases, people do not think about selling their domain name until someone contacts them directly with a purchase offer. If this happens to you — and you do not need the domain name — selling at the right price may hand you an unexpected financial windfall.

Table 11-1   Domain Name Sales Prices, January–September 2000*

Price Range	Percentage of Names Selling in This Range
Less than $5,000	54 percent
$5,000–$100,000	41 percent
Over $100,000	4 percent

*Based on GreatDomains.com sales data

Timing is everything

Like the real estate market, the domain name resale market is likely to go up and down depending on the health of the Internet economy. We've all seen the recent swings in Internet-related stock prices. **Remember:** A domain name is only worth what someone is willing to pay for it. Clearly, domain names sell for higher prices when money is pouring into dot-com businesses instead of pulling out of them. To get a sense of how the larger economy may be affecting domain name prices, keep an eye on key indicators of Internet-related growth. These include

✔ Revenues and earnings growth for Internet infrastructure and application companies

✔ Growth in Internet-related commerce

✔ Growth of Internet use in other countries

Getting an Appraisal

Before you put your domain name on the market, you need to determine how much it is worth. If you don't have an accurate estimate of how much your domain name is worth, you may find yourself asking far too much for an Internet address that never sells as a result — or accepting too little for a name that could sell for more.

In Chapter 10, we cover specific measures that can help you assess the value of your domain name property. The proprietary GreatDomains.com four C valuation process can give you an excellent sense of what your Internet address may be worth. You can also turn to a number of online domain name appraisal service for both quick and in-depth, professional valuations, generally ranging in price from $10 to $75. Keep in mind that the most valid appraisals are based on a large database of comps, or comparable sales. So when you choose an appraiser, consider the depth of their available sales data. Some appraisal services include:

✔ **DomainActions** (www.domainactions.com)

✔ **DomainAppraise** (www.domainappraise.com)

✔ **DomainSystem** (www.solutionhome.com/appraisal)

✔ **GreatDomains.com** (www.greatdomains.com/services/appraisal/appraisalinfo.asp)

✔ **honestdomains.com** (www.honestdomains.com/appraise.htm)

✔ **WebmasterExpert** (www.webmasterexpert.com/domainappraise.htm)

Looking at the Different Ways You Can Sell Your Domain Name

When it comes to selling your domain name, you have several different options. Which option you choose may depend on how you decide to sell in the first place, but read on to find out more and choose the path that's right for you.

Using a domain name broker

In the real-world real estate market, some people list their home "for sale by owner." Many, however, choose to use the services of a real estate broker to help them list their home, find a buyer, and facilitate the sale. The same is true of the domain name market. You can list, promote, and sell a name yourself or you can use the services of one of many domain name brokers.

The most comprehensive brokers will help you appraise your domain name, find a legitimate buyer, represent you in negotiations, handle the contract process, facilitate escrow and re-registration, and help close the deal. Some brokers, such as GreatDomains.com, do substantial marketing and advertising to drive potential buyers to their sites. On-staff account executives may also actively market premium names to potential buyers.

Although most brokers charge a commission (usually 10 to 15 percent of the sales price), the extra money they can make you on your domain name — and the hassles they can save you — may well be worth the fee. Domain name brokers offering a wide range of services include:

- ✔ **BoxDomains** (www.boxdomains.com)
- ✔ **Domain Name Brokers** (www.domainnamebrokers.com)
- ✔ **DomainSell.com** (www.domainsell.com)
- ✔ **GreatDomains.com** (www.greatdomains.com)
- ✔ **URLMerchant** (www.urlmerchant.com)
- ✔ **YourDomain.Org** (www.abcinfo.com/yourdoma.htm)

Working with a buyer who approaches you directly

Many people do not even consider selling their domain name until someone takes the initiative to contact them with an offer to purchase the name. This possibility, of course, is one very good reason why you should always make sure that your contact information in the whois database is up-to-date. If you have moved or changed your e-mail address, a potential buyer will not be able to locate you and make a purchase offer — leaving you without potential profits you could have put in your pocket after a domain name sale.

What is your best strategy if a buyer contacts you directly? Here are the basic steps to increase the odds of a successful sales transaction:

1. **Think about why you may or may not want to keep your domain name.**

   If you are using it for an active Web site, giving it up — even for a fair amount of money — may set back your business, especially if you have to start over and attract visitors to a new Internet address. By the same token, if you are planning to use the name to start an active Web site, selling it may not make the most long-term sense. If, on the other hand, you are not using the name, or if the name means relatively little to your business, then selling it — for the right price — may be a smart decision.

2. **Consider using a domain name broker to represent you.**

   A broker can protect you by validating buyer information, ensuring that you receive a market-value sales price for your name, and providing a controlled transaction process.

3. **Get your domain name appraised.**

   Getting an appraisal is the only way to know your domain name's market value — and the only way you can make sound judgments about potential offers. You can get a ballpark estimate of the name's value by using the valuation process in Chapter 10, or you can pay for a professional appraisal through one of the many online services (see the "Getting an Appraisal" section earlier in this chapter).

4. **Let the buyer make the first offer.**

   This is the most advantageous strategy for a seller. If the appraised value of your domain name, for example, is $7,500 and the buyer offers $5,000, you can then counter higher — at $10,000, for instance — knowing that you will likely be able to negotiate your way to the assessed figure. If, on the other hand, your appraised value is $3,000 and the buyer offers $5,000, you should probably move quickly to close the deal!

5. **Exchange confirmation e-mails detailing all the points and terms of the agreement.**

   These e-mails typically function as an *agreement to agree*. Keep in mind, though, that an exchange of e-mail messages could verbally constitute an actual agreement, so be careful that you don't unintentionally enter in any binding contracts. Also, be aware that the deal can still fall apart for a variety of reasons.

6. **Bring in an escrow company to facilitate the sale.**

   By using a neutral, third-party escrow company to prepare contracts, collect the funds, and oversee the domain name transfer process, you can help ensure that the sale is safe and legal for both you and the buyer. For more details about the escrow process, see Chapter 9.

   Do not spend your domain name profits until you have the buyer's money sitting in your checking account. Plenty of things can still cause the deal to fall through before it is finalized.

7. **Fill out the Registrant Name Change Agreement (RNCA).**

   To transfer the domain name to its new owner, you must complete this paperwork, which is available through many registrars at no charge or for a $35 fee. For more details on the RNCA, see Chapter 9.

8. **Pay all the selling costs.**

   These expenses, which are normally paid by the seller, can include brokerage and escrow fees, legal fees, and miscellaneous out-of-pocket expenses, such as long-distance telephone calls. In some cases, you may be able to negotiate with the buyer to share some of the costs.

Listing your name with "for sale by owner" sites

If you want to take an active approach to marketing your name — without the help of a commission broker — there are many approaches you can take to list your domain name property, publicize it, and increase its chances of selling in the Internet marketplace.

There are dozens of sites on the Internet where you can list your domain name for sale at no charge. If a potential buyer wants to make an offer on your name, he will usually contact you directly through these site, and the two of you will independently negotiate the sale. Many of these services charge a 10 percent commission if the domain name sells through their listing. Some of the many "For Sale by Owner" listing sites include:

- ✔ **AllFreeDomains.com** (www.allfreedomains.com)
- ✔ **ComBuys.com** (www.combuys.com)
- ✔ **MightyDomains.com** (www.mightydomains.com/sell.htm)
- ✔ **TargetDomain.com** (www.targetdomain.com)

Provided that you are not dealing with an exclusive listing service, it is a good idea to list your name with as many resellers as possible. Some of these sites, however, list hundreds or thousands of domain names for sale. So if you want to increase your name's exposure, a number of them will enable you to obtain premium placement for a fee.

Selling a domain name through the negotiated offer process

An alternative to "for sale by owner" sites — through which potential buyers contact sellers directly to work out all the details of a sale — are other sites, such as GreatDomains.com and URLMerchant, which use the *negotiated offer process.* In this type of service, the listing company serves as a mediator between the buyer and seller, facilitating the negotiating process.

As with "for sale by owner" sites, there is no charge to list a domain name with the service, but a percentage of the sale price is charged as a commission if the domain name sells through the site. In addition, there may also be escrow fees for properly transferring the registration, establishing a trust account for the sales proceeds during escrow, and providing appropriate disclosures to protect all parties during the transaction.

Here's how negotiated bidding works through GreatDomains.com.

1. **Go to** www.greatdomains.com **and click on "New Users Join Now."**

   The New Account screen appears.

2. **Fill in your contact information, and select a user ID and password.**

3. **Read the User Agreement, and click on "Create Account."**

   The Welcome to GreatDomains.com screen appears.

4. **Click on "Sell a Domain."**

5. **Enter your domain name, click on "Yes" if your site is already developed, and enter your asking price.**

   It is best to base this price about 20 percent above the appraised value of your name to leave room for negotiating. GreatDomains.com automatically sets the minimum offer at $300.

6. **Type in a description of your domain name.**

   Use this space to list a number of possible uses of your domain name. For example, a description of the domain name "4-movies.com" may read, "Great name for video, television, film, movie, and DVD businesses; rental outlets; production companies; and film industry services."

7. **Type in a list of keywords.**

   Use this space to list as many keywords as possible so that your domain name will appear frequently when people search different domain name categories. For "4-movies.com," the list of keywords may include: movies, film, TV, television, rental, DVD, video, comedy, drama, action, suspense, production, actors, theatrical, performance, locations, scouting, agents, e-commerce, sales.

8. **Review and accept the listing agreement.**

9. **Select the category placement of your name.**

   To increase your domain name's exposure, you can choose from four different levels of placement, at a range of costs. The higher your property is placed in the catalog, the more views it will receive. You also have the ability to place your property in more than one category. The more versatile your name, the more categories you can place it in. The placement choices are:

   - **Lower Level:** This is the cost-free, basic listing. Your domain name will appear at the deepest level of the list. For a nominal charge, you can place your domain name at the top of these free listings.

   - **Third Level:** With this choice, your domain name will appear in the list after a potential buyer clicks through the top and second levels.

   - **Second Level:** This placement lists your domain name in a specific category that you select.

   - **Top Level:** This premium placement exposes your domain name to the most traffic and page views.

   To navigate to lower levels of placement, simply click on a category name — for example, "Entertainment," then "Movies and Film."

10. **When you've made your placement selection, click on "Check Out."**

11. **When a buyer makes an offer, GreatDomains.com will confirm it and then e-mail you the bid amount.**

    At this point, the negotiating process starts.

12. **Negotiate the price.**

    You have 72 hours to accept, decline, or counter the offer. If you decide to counter it, the buyer has the opportunity to accept the counteroffer or counter again. For example, if you have listed your domain name with the asking price of $2,000, and the buyer made an initial offer of $1,500, you may counter with $1,900. The buyer may decline the counter, accept it, or counteroffer again — with, for example, an offer of $1,750.

13. **Close the deal.**

    If you accept the offer, an escrow representative will contact you to take you through the escrow and domain name transfer process. At this point, you are in a binding contract to sell your domain name. In many cases, the entire negotiated offer process can be completed in one day, or there may be as many as six to eight counteroffers over a period of several days.

14. **Transfer the domain name by completing the Registrant Name Change Agreement (RNCA).**

Using the "Fast Sale" model

As an alternative to the standard negotiated offer process, you can also choose to sell your name through a fixed pricing model offered by GreatDomains.com. This process enables sellers to list a domain name for sale at a nonnegotiable, fixed price between $300 and $10,000. The fixed-price model allows for quicker, simpler buyer and seller interaction, as well as speedier escrow and ownership transfer procedures. This approach can reduce the time it takes to complete a domain name sale transaction from eight weeks to two weeks.

Auctioning off your domain name

Another option for selling your domain name is to list it for sale on an auction site. One point to keep in mind, however, is that the auction model works best when there is more than one interested buyer, so that the bidding is competitive. In the case of domain names, however, there is rarely more than one potential buyer per name at any given point in time, so the advantages of selling your name at auction are less clear.

Nevertheless, there are many domain name auction sites on the Internet, including:

- **Afternic.com** (www.afternic.com)
- **ChoiceFree.com** (www.choicefree.com)
- **TheDomainAuction.com** (www.thedomainauction.com)
- **DomainSystems** (www.solutionhome.com)
- **Dot Broker** (www.dotbroker.com)
- **eBay** (www.ebay.com, or see domain name listings at listings.ebay.com/aw/listings/list/all/category3767)
- **ezDomainAuction** (www.ezdomainauction.com)
- **NamesForBid.com** (www.namesforbid.com)
- **ShoutLoud.com** (www.shoutloud.com)
- **Yahoo!Auctions** (auctions.yahoo.com, or see domain name listings at auctions.yahoo.com/27751-category-leaf.html)

Although each of these sites has specific rules and procedures, the basic auction selling process works like this:

1. **Register or join the auction site as a user.**

   On most sites, you register under the "Getting Started" or "Register" heading. In most cases, registering entails reading and accepting a user service agreement, entering your credit card information, and providing your e-mail address, a user name, and a password of your choice.

2. **Pay a fee, if necessary.**

   Some sites charge a small fee to complete the registration process.

3. **Select the type of auction you wish to hold.**

   These can include:

   - **"Make Offer" auctions,** in which you solicit offers at the same time that you put your domain name up for sale at a fixed asking price. The auction ends when you accept a buyer's offer or a buyer accepts your asking price.

   - **Consignment auctions,** which begin only when the first bid is placed and continue for a duration that you select.

   - **Fixed-length auctions,** which begin immediately, with or without an initial bid, and end on the closing date you specify.

4. **List and describe the name that you wish to sell.**

   As with other listing sites, be sure to briefly indicate all the possible uses for your domain name.

5. **Select the categories in which you want your domain name to be listed, such as "Business," "Consumer Goods," or "Entertainment."**

6. **Set your reserve price and indicate whether you wish to reveal the reserve price to potential buyers.**

   The *reserve price* is the lowest bid that you will accept for your domain name. If bidding does not reach the reserve price, you have no obligation to sell the name. Setting a low reserve price can be a good strategy in order to spark interest in the auction.

7. **Name your starting price.**

   The *starting price* is the minimum amount that anyone can offer when a domain name auction starts. Setting a low starting price is a good idea. If you don't specify a starting price, some sites will set this figure automatically at a small percentage of the reserve price.

8. **Specify the duration of your auction.**

   On some sites, this can range from 1 to 30 days; on others, the auction length may range from 2 or 3 days to 10 days in length.

9. **Promote your auction.**

   Some auction sites enable you to enhance the visibility of your domain name by paying for premium placement at the top of category listings. In some cases, you can also draw attention by listing your domain name in boldface type and adding color and design elements to your description.

10. Monitor your auction.

Many sites enable you to track your auction activity by clicking on a simple link. You can usually make changes to an auction or remove your domain name from an auction listing only if no one has met the starting bid.

If no one meets your reserve price by the time a fixed-length auction ends, there is no winner. At that point, if you choose, you can resubmit your domain name to the site for listing in another auction.

If there is a successful high bidder in your auction, some sites notify you by e-mail. You and the seller should then move into the escrow process (which we discuss earlier in this chapter) and complete the transfer of the domain name registration. Some sites provide services and online tools to facilitate closing procedures. On many sites, however, the buyer and seller are responsible for contacting each other and working out the payment and transfer process on their own.

Keep copies of all documentation, including printed copies of electronic records of all bids, agreements, payments, and other auction information. Auction sites will not provide these documents for you.

Promoting Your Domain Name

To increase the likelihood that your domain name will sell — whether you use a "for sale by owner" site, a negotiated offer, or an auction listing site — promoting it and letting people know that the name is for sale is a smart move. You can promote your domain name in many ways. For the most part, you are limited only by your own financial budget and your imagination.

In this section, we look at a number of promotional strategies that can help you find the right buyer for your domain name property — from simple, low-budget options to marketing ideas that require a bigger commitment of both time and money.

Advertising your domain name through a Web page

If a domain name is comparable to undeveloped real estate, then linking that Internet address to a Web site is like putting up a building on the property, thereby increasing its value. When you are selling a domain name, at the very least you should consider linking it to a promotional Web page — the equivalent of putting a "for sale" sign or a billboard on a piece of land that you want to sell.

In many cases, you can put up a simple, one-page promotional site for free through a listing site. At GreatDomains.com, for example, you can create a "free parking" page that will automatically be seen by anyone who types your domain name into his browser bar. You can also set up a free or inexpensive Web page through domain name registrars such as Network Solutions and register.com.

Your promotional Web page should ideally include the following information:

- ✔ A banner headline featuring the domain name and announcing that it is up for sale
- ✔ A short paragraph indicating what types of buyers and businesses would benefit from the domain name
- ✔ A short paragraph about the benefits of the name — what features make it attractive and appealing
- ✔ Your asking price
- ✔ Acceptable forms of payment
- ✔ Your contact information

Writing a press release

If there is something unusual or intriguing about the domain name you are selling, you could also write and send out a press release that promotes it to targeted publications and news sources. For example, if you are trying to sell the domain name Buydowntownseattle.com with an asking price of $5,000, you could write and send out a press release that reads:

> Buy Downtown Seattle for $5,000!
>
> Business leaders in the market for hot virtual real estate now have an exceptional opportunity. An Internet entrepreneur, YOUR NAME, is offering the prime domain name Buydowntownseattle.com for sale for only $5,000.
>
> Perfect for Seattle commercial and residential realtors, as well as local, retail-related portals, this premium Internet property has great development potential. For more information, contact YOUR NAME at YOUR CONTACT INFORMATION.

Keep in mind that chances of getting press coverage of your domain name are slim unless there is something particularly timely, unusual, or newsworthy about your story.

You can distribute your press release yourself, at relatively little cost, by mailing it to a targeted list of newspapers and other publications that you compile yourself. Although a more costly alternative, you can use paid news distribution services such as:

- ✔ **Go Press Release** (www.gopressrelease.com)
- ✔ **Press Release Network** (www.pressreleasenetwork.com)

Launching an e-mail campaign

Another promotional strategy is to e-mail a "for sale" announcement about your domain name to the relevant decision makers at companies that may be potential purchasers. For example, to market the domain name 4-movies.com, you could send an e-mail about the name, its attractive features, and its price to a list of companies in the video and film industry.

You can also hire the services of domain name marketing companies to help you do this, such as:

- ✔ **CornerStone International** (www.CornerStone.OnTheWeb.nu)
- ✔ **DomainPromoters.com** (www.domainpromoters.com)

Buying ads in related trade magazines

If you have a premium domain name that you believe may sell for a high price to an interested business, you may want to consider placing an advertisement in a trade magazine, newsletter, or other publication that targets that particular industry. Although this can be a relatively expensive option, it may be a worthwhile investment for the right type of domain name.

Going to trade shows

Another option for promoting a premium domain name is to go to related trade shows and pass out stickers, flyers, and other materials that creatively market your name.

In addition to industry-specific trade shows, you can market your domain name at Internet trade shows including:

✔ Fall Internet World (for information, go to `www.pentonevents.com`)

✔ Spring Internet World (see `www.pentonevents.com` for information)

✔ Comdex (go to `www.key3media.com` for details)

Attending trade shows can be a relatively expensive strategy — considering travel and material costs — but for a valuable name, the visibility could turn out to be worthwhile.

Keeping in Mind Some Key Points on Selling Your Domain Name

Before you go ahead and put your domain name up for sale, here are a few last words of advice:

✔ **Do not set your expectations too high.** Even though some domain names have sold for millions, most sell for far less than that, so think hard before you turn down a reasonable offer. Of course, the best way to judge whether an offer is reasonable is to have your domain name appraised — that way, you will have the information that you need to make the best decisions.

✔ **Never let your domain name registration expire**. If you forget to renew your registration, your title to the name will lapse. In that case, you may find yourself trying to sell a domain name that no longer belongs to you.

Chapter 12

Renting Out Your Domain Name

● ●

In This Chapter

▶ Making a fortune by subdividing domain name properties

▶ Renting out domain name billboard space

● ●

*T*he right domain name can be a smart investment for any individual or company wanting a prime location on the Internet. And it can mean substantial profits for those who sell their domain names for considerably more than the $35, $70, or $100 that they spent to register them. Internet entrepreneurs have reaped big profits in the domain name game by thinking ahead of the curve and coming up with innovative moneymaking strategies.

In this chapter, we look at two of these success stories — how entrepreneurial investors have turned domain names into fortunes by subdividing and renting out their valuable virtual real estate instead of selling it outright. Although these successful strategies may not be duplicated in the fast-changing domain name marketplace, creative Internet entrepreneurs will undoubtedly be able to seize on new opportunities that arise as the virtual real estate market matures.

Subdividing Domain Name Property

For Canadian entrepreneur Jerry Sumpton — founder of Mailbank.com — the secret to domain name success has been the rental concept. In Sumpton's case, he has done the domain name equivalent of putting a rental apartment building on each piece of valuable Internet real estate that he owns. The result has been a multimillion-dollar business success story.

Mailbank, which Sumpton sold control of in 1999, owns over 14,000 domain names, including many family names such as Smith.net, Gibson.org, and Ramirez.com. The company's Internet addresses, in fact, represent the last names of about 60 percent of the population of the United States. Mailbank makes its money by subdividing those domain name properties and renting them out as e-mail addresses (such as `tina@smith.net`) and Web sites addresses (such as `www.tina.smith.net`). Mailbank also offers affinity-related domain names (such as Tennisplayers.com, Ballerinas.com, TheEngineer.com, and ChessMasters.com), which it rents out to customers in the same way.

With just under 100,000 customers in about 100 countries — gained with a minimum of marketing — Mailbank has created a profitable strategy for developing and maximizing its extensive domain name assets.

Jerry Sumpton got started in the domain name business as a computer consultant in Vancouver, Canada. He registered his first domain name — Freeview.com — in September 1995 as the name for an online horse-brokerage Internet business that he planned to start. Soon, however, he became convinced that domain names themselves would be increasingly valuable assets — so, with the help of investors, he quickly registered 500 Internet addresses related to activities like jobs, pets, and hobbies.

It was clear to Sumpton that most of the really good names were already disappearing fast. So in 1996 he had the idea of registering family-related domain names. Even at that stage, Sumpton said, he planned to hold onto the domain name property that he was buying. "I saw it as a domain name development business," he explained. "I didn't want to flip the names, selling them at a profit. Instead, I wanted to add value to the domain names I acquired and keep them as long-term assets."

Before he began accumulating the family names, however, Sumpton had to figure out which ones he should purchase as an investment. Using commercially available CDs of white-page telephone-book listings for the United States and Canada, Sumpton counted all the unique family names, totaling about 1.5 million. Out of that huge pool of names, Sumpton found that just 7,500 last names represented 70 percent of the population.

With that key list of names in hand, Sumpton started registering as many domain names as he could, 500 to 600 at a time — at the high price, back then, of $100 each. "I was working 8- to 12-hour days, 7 days a week, just registering domain names, writing software to start the business, and scrounging to raise cash," Sumpton recalls.

In July 1996, his new company, Mailbank, started renting e-mail addresses for an annual fee. Within two months, he had customers in 60 different countries. Business came to him through a simple, low-cost marketing approach. When people, roaming the Internet, typed their last names into their browser bar, a Web site would come up, in many cases, telling them about Mailbank's services. In 1997, Mailbank also started offering related Web addresses for rent — and, according to Tom Savage, Mailbank's current CEO, the business is poised for future growth. "By renting an Internet address from Mailbank," he said, "our customers have a simple, personalized identity that is intuitive and easy to remember." With stepped-up marketing, he said, they can realize a lot of untapped potential.

The most popular family domains

Based on Mailbank's business experience, the company's five most popular "family" domain names in the United States and Canada are, in order:

1. Smith.net

2. Johnson.org

3. Brown.org

4. Wilson.org

5. Thomas.net

A few other companies are offering similar domain name rental services. Mail.com, for instance, owns several hundred prime affinity- and location-related domain names for e-mail addresses, including USA.com, Catlover.com, London.com, and Archaeologist.com. Mailbank, however, has the corner on family name Internet addresses. With the release of the new TLDs, however, the field may well open up to a whole new crop of savvy domain name developers.

Renting Virtual Billboard Space

Creative domain name entrepreneurs have also earned millions through other innovative online opportunities. Rick Schwartz, for instance, an "Internet real estate developer" in Boca Raton, Florida, has parlayed the 3,000 domain names he owns into a multimillion-dollar virtual billboard business. Like Mailbank, Schwartz is not interested in selling any of his names, although he said he has received offers on many of them. "I have ideas for developing them all at some point," he explained. "But even without selling them, they pump out over $3 million a year in profit," he noted, in billboard advertising revenues alone.

It works like this. One of Schwartz's sites, Ebid.com, has nothing on it but an advertising banner. The ad links visitors to an active auction site that pays Schwartz to display the banner. Even though Ebid.com has essentially no content but the ad, Schwartz's site still gets 1,500 hits a day from people who are hunting for Web auctions and randomly typing Ebid.com into their browser bars. Of course, Ebid.com would be a great name for a full-fledged auction Web site — but as a virtual billboard, in a prime location on the information highway, it has turned into pure gold.

Of the 1,500 visitors a day who stop at Ebid.com, fully 40 percent of them — some 60 people a day, or 18,000 people a month — click on the advertising banner. And fully 25 percent of those individuals, Schwartz said, actually sign up for the advertiser's services. For supplying all that traffic to several sponsors on his site, Schwartz makes over $1,000 a day on that one site alone. "It's like an oil well," he asserted. Collectively, Schwartz's 3,000 sites receive more than 3.5 million unique visitors a month, making them very attractive properties for advertisers.

To expand his portfolio of domain names, Schwartz regularly browses the Internet, purchasing names such as Publicopinionpoll.com for $3,500 or a collection of 150 names beginning with the word *virtual,* such as Virtualdoctor.com, Virtualmuseum.com, and Virtualcardealer.com. His most valuable domain name properties, he believes, are those such as Wholesalefurniture.com and Wholesalejewelry.com that, he said, "represent an instant business" — one he may develop himself or promote using the domain name as a billboard. Though many of his domain names are linked to adult sites, Schwartz has also positioned himself to have market share in dozens of different industries.

Nothing, in his belief, can match the potential of the domain name marketplace. "A prime dot-com domain will go up in value faster than any property ever known to man," he predicted. "No stock on the stock market has outperformed my domain names, because the traffic that they generate is unbelievable. I have at least 100,000 new visitors to my sites every day. That's enough people to fill up Yankee Stadium twice a day — with no advertising. Not even the Yankees," Schwartz declared, "can do that."

Although making a lot of money through Internet-based advertising is getting harder — especially now that so many of the premium domain names are gone — there are opportunities to earn revenue through advertising so long as your domain name and Web site attract a significant amount of traffic. Lots of traffic-building and advertising tips are available on the Internet. If you're interested, check out these sites for starters:

- ✔ **Bizpromo** (www.bizpromo.com/free/10traffic.htm)
- ✔ **MyComputer.com** (www.mycomputer.com)
- ✔ **reallybig.com** (reallybig.com/reallybig.shtml)
- ✔ **Web Site Garage** (websitegarage.netscape.com)

Part VI
Buying and Selling Web Sites

The 5th Wave   By Rich Tennant

MCSE TCP/IP TESTING

"I assume you'll be forward thinking enough to allow '.dog' as a valid domain name."

In this part . . .

*1*f what you really want is a Web site that's already in existence — and not just the domain name attached to it — you've come to the right place. Here we guide you through the process of valuing a Web site, so you know you're not paying more for a site than it's really worth. We also let you know how you can profit from your Web site by selling it to someone else. Finally, we give you some very helpful information on selling your entire Web-based business, which is a bit different from selling just a Web site or a domain name.

Chapter 13

Understanding the New Resale
Market for Web Sites

In This Chapter

▶ Knowing where the marketplace has been and where it's going

▶ Figuring out what you can expect — whether you're planning to buy or sell

*T*he growth of the Internet — as well as the release of the new TLDs — has been fueling the fast-growing domain name resale market. The next wave of business opportunity on the Net, however, may be the buying and selling of Web-based business sites.

Since the "land rush" for Internet locations began, entrepreneurs have raced to develop their virtual property — creating thousands of Web sites specializing in content and e-commerce for the consumer and business markets. Many have built significant value by developing Web site technology, creating valuable content and strong databases, generating sound revenue and income streams, and establishing business relationships with valuable partners.

On the other hand, given the heady atmosphere — and low barriers to entry — of this new business frontier, many other sites were put up without sound business models and financial plans. As a result, many of these sites, once wildly overvalued, have recently been going out of business.

As the Internet marketplace matures, nonetheless, there are still thousands of valuable sites on the Web — many with substantial traffic and viable business models — that will quietly survive the turmoil in the brand new online marketplace. If you're interested in getting into the Web market or enhancing your existing online offerings with additional features and services, these solid properties may be a valuable investment. In this chapter, we look at the potential of the new resale market for Web sites and Web-based businesses and let you know how you can get involved.

Hindsight Is 20/20: Making Sure You Don't Repeat the Past Mistakes of Those Who've Gone Before You

In the early days of online business, there were few rules, few standards, and often unreasonably high expectations of success. Setting up a Web site is relatively easy and inexpensive. Thousands of people did so assuming that the sheer number of people surfing the Net would instantly deliver profits to their online bottom line. To lure those visitors, many people spent huge budgets on marketing and advertising, even though their actual online business lacked many of the basic fundamentals that it takes to satisfy and retain customers.

In other words, you can open an expensively designed store in a highly trafficked shopping mall and spend a fortune on advertising it in magazines, in newspapers, and on TV. But if you're selling things that nobody wants to buy — and if your customer service does not make the cut — you probably won't stay in business for long.

That, in fact, is what has happened in the great Web-based business shakeout. Many of those companies that had inflated expectations of making a huge amount of money fast by tapping the Internet market or going public have been disappointed. Putting a business on the Internet may be relatively easy, but making it successful is no easier on the Internet than building a winning business in the physical, bricks-and-mortar marketplace is.

Buying In to the Web Site Marketplace

Despite the numerous examples of failed online businesses, there are plenty of Web-based enterprises out there launched by people with solid business ideas, a good understanding of their customers, and relatively low expenses. But they may be operated out of people's homes and marketed through good search-engine placements instead of multimillion-dollar advertising budgets.

Many of these successful Web sites may be turning out a slim profit with relatively little effort. Although they are not necessarily making any headlines, they may have the potential to be considerably more profitable after the Internet marketplace weeds out a lot of their competition.

Think of it this way: Imagine that 50 bookstores are located on one university campus, all competing to sell books to the faculty and students. Most likely, not a single store is making good money, even though the demand for books is high, because the marketplace is oversaturated. Soon enough, most of those 50 bookstores will eventually go out of business, however, leaving perhaps three remaining stores. And those surviving bookstores will proba-bly be very successful, because the demand for books is strong, growing, and easily large enough to support them.

In some ways, the same thing is happening with Internet commerce right now. The market is oversaturated, and the sites with weaker business models are shutting down. The ones that remain — and that continue to grow and improve with time — will be very well positioned for success in the next phase of the e-commerce revolution.

If you're interested in buying a Web-based business instead of building one — and if you have the patience to develop the business on your own over the next few years without expecting to generate big profits fast — this could actually be an exceptionally good time to make a deal.

With the value of so many Web sites declining, many owners may be open to a reasonable offer. If you buy a promising Web business and hold on to it — building traffic and customer loyalty while keeping your expenses low — you could end up with a big winner in a few years when the marketplace grows and matures.

Putting Your Best Foot Forward When You Get Ready to Sell

Although buyers today may have attractive opportunities when it comes to Web sites, sellers, unfortunately, face a tougher challenge. With the Web site resale market just being born and the value of so many properties plunging, there are fewer potential buyers out there than site owners willing to sell. And that means that it's a buyer's market.

But take heart. By holding onto your Web enterprise, strengthening its strat-egy for generating revenues and profits, building your traffic, and developing a base of loyal, repeat customers, you can increase the value of your Web site over time and greatly boost your odds of selling it for a fair price.

Building revenues and profits

You may have a Web site that attracts a lot of visitors, but unless you are able to turn that traffic into sales dollars, you may have a hard time finding a buyer for your site. To make your site more attractive to potential pur-chasers, look for ways that you can generate sales revenues and profits over the Web. For example, if you have a Web site that offers extensive information on bike riding — from equipment to training and travel tips — consider sell-ing bikes, accessories, and other related items online to your target market.

Increasing traffic

Great online traffic may not be all you need to attract a buyer for your Web site, but it is still a crucial feature. Think of it this way — if you are a store owner, you will have lots of opportunities for sales if crowds of people come into your store everyday. On the other hand, if people hardly ever walk through the door, your revenue potential will be much more limited. The same is very true on the Web. By building your traffic, you build your potential for sales and profits — and make your site much more attractive to buyers.

There are a variety of tools and services available to you on the Web to help you increase traffic to your site. These include:

- **Microsoft bCentral.com** (www.bcentral.com), a site that offers a software product called Traffic Builder to help you drive potential customers to your online business.

- **Advertising.com** (www.advertising.com/expertise/action.html), a service that helps you increase Web traffic through online advertising.

Developing a loyal customer base

The best online customers are repeat customers. If you have a large base of loyal users, your site will be more appealing to buyers. One way of increasing the number of visitors who come back to your Web site again and again is to stay in touch with them regularly. Here's how:

- When users first visit your site, have them fill out a membership information form that asks for an e-mail address.

- Every time you introduce a new service, product, or feature, send a promotional e-mail to all your members reminding them to visit your Web site.

- Take advantage of one of the companies, such as Doubleclick.net (www.doubleclick.net), that offer e-mail marketing services that can help you drive repeat business from existing customers and members.

- Turn your Web site into an online community by adding chat room and forum features that encourage your visitors to come back and interact time after time.

- Feature news items and links on your site that will interest your users and update them regularly to keep those visitors coming back.

By the numbers

The resale market for Web sites is likely to grow quickly as Web use continues to expand. According to Dun and Bradstreet, small business use of the Internet to purchase goods and services for business use rose from 38 percent in 1998 to 43 percent in 1999. And consider the statistics in the following table for proof that the Internet is growing by leaps and bounds.

Form of Internet Use	Percentage of People Using the Internet for This Purpose in 1998	Percentage of People Using the Internet for This Purpose in 2000
Shop online	31 percent	56 percent
Intend to shop online in the future	14 percent	28 percent
Plan to increase online purchases	41 percent	49 percent
Conduct banking activities	16 percent	25 percent
Trade stocks	11 percent	16 percent

Source: AOL/Roper Starch Cyberstudy

The top ten Web properties

Traffic is one of the keys to building the value of a Web site. Who is doing it right? According to Media Metrix, these were the ten Web sites drawing the greatest number of unique visitors in September 2000:

Ranking	Property	Unique Visitors (In Thousands)
1	AOL Network	60,988
2	Yahoo!	52,679
3	Microsoft Sites	51,425
4	Lycos	30,780
5	Excite Network	26,958
6	Go Network	22,987
7	About.com Sites	20,637
8	AltaVista	19,249
9	Time Warner Online	15,865
10	Amazon	15,294

Chapter 14

Buying an Existing Web Site

• •

In This Chapter

▶ Figuring out whether you should buy a Web site

▶ Knowing how to find a Web site for sale

▶ Engaging in the due diligence process

▶ Coming up with a fair offer

• •

*A*nyone who has ever played the classic Parker Brothers board game *Monopoly* knows that a prime piece of property — like Park Place — is worth even more when it has a house or a hotel on it. The same is true in the Internet real estate game. Buying a domain name is like purchasing a piece of undeveloped property, hopefully in a premium location. Buying a Web site, on the other hand, is like buying a piece of property that has a developed business on it. In a Web site purchase, you acquire both assets — the location or domain name and the improvements and profit-making potential that have already been developed on that site. Although buying a Web site may not make you a cyber-real-estate baron, it will give you virtual assets over and above the domain name that you can then develop further and profit from in the future.

Because business assets are often involved, however, purchasing a Web site is a pretty complicated matter that has a lot in common with buying a company in the bricks-and-mortar world. Don't attempt to complete a transaction like this without good legal and accounting advice. In the case of a Web site purchase, the advice of a technical expert can be very valuable, too.

That said, buying a Web site may make a lot of sense for individuals who want to take advantage of a full- or part-time small business opportunity — and for existing companies that want to expand their marketing reach without going though the time-consuming process of designing and setting up their own Web site from scratch. In this chapter, we look at how to find a Web site that is for sale, important factors to consider when making a purchasing decision, and the process of making a deal.

Considering Reasons for Buying a Web Site

Buying an existing Web site may be a sound business decision for individuals or companies that want to save development time and get their business onto the Net quickly. Reasons for purchasing a Web site may include:

✔ **Turning an expertise or hobby into a business.** If, for example, you are an expert in fly fishing or model ships, you may want to take that hobby and turn it into a viable part-time business by purchasing an existing Web site that already provides products, services, and information to your targeted customers.

✔ **Eliminating competition.** If you already have an active Internet-based business, you can eliminate a competitor whose site is on the market by purchasing that online business.

✔ **Capturing market share.** A business can also expand its customer base by buying a Web site that reaches its targeted market. By adding that site to its existing virtual or bricks-and-mortar enterprise, a business can instantly add that key traffic to its base.

✔ **Acquiring technology.** In some cases, a Web site may be valuable to a particular business because of its unique proprietary technology. Purchasing the site can give a company the technology it needs to grow without having to spend the time it would take to develop that capability independently.

Knowing What Type of Web Site to Buy

Although many Web sites operate primarily as promotional tools that offer minimal information and depend mainly on advertising for revenues, those with the most commercial value are often e-commerce sites that enable visitors to buy products or services online.

Some examples of Web sites that fit this business model include:

✔ A site that markets specialized products, such as equipment and accessories for home baking customers

✔ A site that offers general and product-specific information — such as content related to valuable coins — as well as online sales of related products

✔ A site that features a searchable database and online transactions — such as one that specializes in skiing vacations, with online searching of resorts, hotels, and travel information, as well as secure purchases of travel and other related products

If you already have an existing online business and want to attract additional traffic, another type of Web site that may be valuable to you is a site that features a wealth of original content and draws a high number of your potential customers. For example, if you sell videos or feature films over the Web, it may make a lot of sense for you to acquire another site that has an extensive, well-trafficked inventory of original movie reviews. By integrating that content — and those visitors — into your site, you can potentially boost the volume of your movie sales.

Figuring Out Whether to Buy or Build a Web Site

If you're interested in starting an online business, one of the first questions you should consider is whether it makes more sense for you to buy an existing site or build your own Web site from scratch. Although buying an active site will usually save you time, it will not necessarily save you money. If you're a do-it-yourselfer with a limited budget and little time pressure, it may make sense for you to create your own site. You can usually do so for less than it would cost to buy one.

Buying an established site does offer these potential advantages:

- **Traffic.** You instantly have access to an existing customer base.

- **Technology.** You gain the benefit of a proven online system.

- **Reduced competition.** By buying a site, you eliminate a potential competitor.

On the other hand, buying a Web site may not be the best way to go if that site is:

- **Too expensive.** You could build a better, more effective site for less money than an existing Web site would cost to buy.

- **Uncompetitive.** The site is a small player in an industry that is increasingly dominated by a big online company that offers customers better service and selection at a lower price.

- **Mired in problems** such as financial, legal, or employee-related liabilities. It is crucial, of course, to uncover any potential problems before you buy a site by performing due diligence in all key areas. (We will look at that process in considerable detail later in this chapter.)

Finding a Web Site That's for Sale

There are two main ways to identify a Web site that is available to purchase: searching a growing number of sites on the Internet that list developed Web sites for sale and searching the Web yourself for sites that interest you.

Turning to listings of Web sites for sale

The Web site resale market is much younger than the secondary domain name market. As a result, most Web site listing services offer fewer features than domain name brokers and resellers. Nevertheless, they can be a good place to start when you are looking for a Web site business to buy.

Online Web site listing services include:

- ✔ **Axiopolis** (www.axiopolis.com)
- ✔ **GreatWebsites.com** (www.greatwebsites.com)
- ✔ **Time2Sell** (www.time2sell.com)
- ✔ **WebSitesBroker.com** (www.websitebroker.com)

Searching on your own for sites you're interested in buying

You can conduct your own search on the Web and look for Web sites that you're interested in buying, whether or not they're for sale. When you have identified a particular site that you may be interested in buying, you need to contact the owner by phone or e-mail indicating your interest in making an offer.

Although e-mail contact usually works well when it comes to buying a domain name, there is an advantage to using the telephone when you are negotiating the purchase of a Web site. Telephone contact, after all, allows you to glean more information about the seller. By his or her tone of voice and immediate responses to your offer, you may be able to gain a more accurate sense of the seller's interest level and personal motivations for considering the sale. All this information should be factored into your negotiating strategy and your ultimate purchasing decision.

Getting Professional Advice Before You Buy

If you've found a Web site owner who is seriously interested in selling the site, the two of you should execute a letter of intent, with as much detail as possible so that there will be few chances for misunderstanding later. Next you, the buyer, should begin gathering information and evaluating the online business to get an accurate picture of its financial, legal, technical, and management situation, as well as key matters such as its technology, content, and traffic.

No buyer should attempt to do this alone, however. These are often complex matters that require specialized knowledge and experience.

Engage the services of a lawyer, an accountant, and perhaps a technical consultant to help you navigate the complex due diligence process (covered in the next section).

Working through the Due Diligence Process

Benjamin Franklin once said, "Diligence is the mother of good luck." When it comes to buying a business, *due diligence* is the process of preventing bad luck by finding out as much as you can about the company — from its financial status and liabilities to its employees and reputation — before you close the deal.

The due diligence process can be relatively straightforward or very complex, depending on the nature of the business you are looking at. Commercial Web sites are in many ways like any brick-and-mortar business. In fact, some Web businesses are combination of the two. For example, a local retail outlet store may also sell its inventory online. In a "clicks-and-mortar" case like this, there are physical and virtual assets and liabilities to assess.

Even with pure Internet enterprises that sell products or services only over the distribution channel of the Net, there are basic areas that you should analyze carefully before purchasing the site. Many of these are the same factors that you would look at in any traditional business, and others are unique to the online marketplace.

Looking at the financials

One very important area to examine carefully (with the help of your accountant) is the financial records of the online business. Specifically, there are two key documents to look at:

- ✔ **The site's balance sheet,** which lists all of the business's financial assets and liabilities
- ✔ **The site's income statement,** which shows its revenues and expenses over a particular period of time

Of course, your accountant should also carefully examine other financial records, including the site's statement of cash flows. For now, however, we take a closer look at what the first two documents can tell you about the site you wish to buy.

Assessing the site's assets and liabilities

The balance sheet is an important document that can help you see, in one page, what a business may be worth and where there may be some hidden problems. Every balance sheet is divided into two sections: assets and liabilities. Of course, the first thing you want to determine is that the liabilities do not exceed the assets. Other than that, there is a lot that you can learn about an online business by looking at these numbers.

Let's take a look, for example, at the hypothetical balance sheet of WonderWidgets.com, a clicks-and-mortar online business that manufactures widgets and sells them over its e-commerce Web site. As a potential buyer of the site, you can find out from the balance sheet that:

- ✔ **The company has enough current assets to pay its current debts.** That is a reassuring sign. You can see in Figure 14-1 that the company's current assets — which can be converted into cash within a year — total $181,174. Looking at the liabilities column in Figure 14-2, you also see its current liabilities — all those debts coming due within a year — add up to $34,480. So far, so good.

- ✔ **The site has a good amount of working capital.** When you subtract WonderWidgets's current liabilities from its current assets, you get $146,694. That amount is called the company's *working capital,* the money it can use to run its business. It seems like this Web site is in good financial shape, at least for the short term.

- ✔ **You need to find out more about WonderWidgets's history with accounts receivable.** The assets column, for example, tells you that the site has $12,679 in accounts receivable. It is hard to draw any conclusions about this number, however, without gathering more information. You need to get the company's balance sheets for the prior two, three, or four years and compare them. Also look at the company's income statements for the same time periods (see Figure 14-3). If you see that the accounts receivables number has been growing at the same time that the site's revenues have been growing, there is little reason to be alarmed. If, on the other hand, the accounts receivables have been growing while revenues have been shrinking, the site could have a fundamental business problem. Maybe, for example, its widgets are no longer as competitive as they once were. In any case, you need to find out the reason why accounts receivable and revenues are trending in opposite directions.

✔ **You need to verify the company's inventory.** WonderWidgets has an inventory that it values at $121,259. It is not typical for a Web site to carry inventory, but a click-and-mortar business like WonderWidgets may keep a stock of its products on hand. If a company does list inventory on its balance sheet, you need to verify that the inventory does, in fact, exist and that it is worth the listed amount. You want to know, for example, that this site's inventory of widgets is not damaged, outdated, or unsalable in some other way. The best way to do this is to hire someone (perhaps through your accounting firm) who can physically go to the premises, count and value the inventory, and make sure that what is reflected on the balance sheet is indeed there in the warehouse.

✔ **The company appears to have relatively new equipment.** When you look at the company's fixed assets in Figure 14-1, you see that it has $163,264 in equipment and fixtures — most probably relating to equipment that the company uses to produce its widgets. The company also has $11,401 in transportation equipment — most likely a truck or company car. The value of these assets declines every year due to wear and tear, and that loss is totaled on the accumulated depreciation line. If the amount of accumulated depreciation comes close to the $174,665 total of the fixed assets, you would know that the company's equipment is pretty old and would probably need to be replaced soon. That would be a major consideration if you were thinking about buying the business. In WonderWidgets's case, however, the accumulated depreciation only totals $66,850. That is good news, because it implies that the company's equipment is reasonably new.

On the liability side, you need to look at the balance sheet to make sure that the current liabilities and long-term debt do not exceed the business's total assets. If the liability number is higher than the asset number, it may be a red flag that the company has not been as careful in taking on debt as it should have been. In the case of WonderWidgets, however, there appears to be no cause for alarm. Total assets are $371,398. Its current liabilities of $34,480 plus its total long-term debt of $67,332 add up to $101,812. That leaves a positive balance of $269,586. The online company looks like it is in good shape.

In the case of WonderWidgets.com, the balance sheet looks very healthy. Current assets exceed current liabilities by a good amount. The fixed assets seem relatively new. Nothing on either the assets or liabilities side appears to raise any serious red flags. It is important, however, to have your accountant look over this balance sheet, and those for prior years, very carefully to get as clear a picture and as much detail as possible about the company's financial situation.

Reviewing revenues and expenses

Another very important document that you need to review is the income statement of the site that is for sale (refer to Figure 14-3). Basically, the income statement is an overview of the company's sales and profits, as well as all the costs that went into production of sales and operating the business. It reports the business's:

- ✔ **Revenues:** The sales of the company during the specified period from e-commerce, advertising, subscriptions, licensing, and other activities.

- ✔ **The cost of goods sold:** Those expenses that went into generating sales, including material costs and salaries.

- ✔ **Operating expenses:** Costs indirectly related to selling the products or services, such as server costs, sales force salaries, car expenses, telephone costs, bandwidth charges, sales office space, desks, chairs, and general equipment and supplies.

Small, privately held companies can be fairly liberal about the operating expenses that they claim. Have your accountant check the details behind these expenses to see if they include items such as personal cars, boats, or vacation homes (used only for business purposes, of course). If these types of items are indeed reflected in the operating expenses — and if they would not be included in the company's sale — your accountant should recalculate the operating expenses without them.

- ✔ **Pretax income:** The amount of money that is left after all costs and expenses have been deducted from revenues. This should be a positive number, indicating that the money coming in to the business exceeds the money going out of it. If the pretax income number is negative, your accountant should look especially carefully at what lies behind the cost of goods sold and operating expenses.

- ✔ **Net income:** The money remaining from revenues after all costs, expenses, and taxes have been deducted (otherwise known as *profit*).

Your accountant should take a close look at the details behind these numbers. The net income should be a positive number. In the case of WonderWidgets, net income (or profit) is $94,429, about 5 percent of revenues. That percentage is the profit margin of the business, and it is a reasonably healthy number.

A Web site business may still be a good purchase even if it does not have a profitable bottom line. It may offer you other important benefits, such as high traffic, unique technology, or the potential for fast growth — factors that you need to take into account when making your purchasing decision.

Wonder Widgets Company

Balance
Sheet

ASSETS
Assests:
Current Assets:

Cash and Equivalents	44,806
Investments	1,850
Accounts Receivable	12,679
Prepaid Expenses	580
Inventory	121,259
Total Current Assets	181,174

Fixed Assets:

Equipment and Fixtures	163,264
Transportation Equipment	11,401
Total Fixed Assets, Cost	174,665
Accumulated Depreciation	(66,850)
Total Fixed Assets, Net	107,815

Other Assets:

Capitalized Leases, Net	47,838
Deferred Taxes	8,833
Miscellaneous Assets	25,738
Total Other Assets	82,409
TOTAL ASSETS	371,398

Figure 14-1:
The assets
as shown on
a balance
sheet.

Compare this income statement with those from previous years. Have your accountant compare the revenues, the costs of goods sold, and the operating expenses in this statement to those in previous years and determine what the percentage of growth or decline in each of those categories has been. If, for example, WonderWidgets's revenues grew at 10 percent over the last two years, while cost of goods sold grew 6 percent and operating expenses grew 3 percent, the business would seem to be in good shape and growing nicely. If, on the other hand, revenues grew 4 percent, while cost of goods sold grew 6 percent and operating expenses grew 12 percent, there could be some fundamental problems with the business that you and your accountant should look into closely.

Don't be surprised if the Web-based business you're looking at does not have a lengthy operating history. Most Web businesses have been in existence for a relatively short time period.

```
                        Wonder Widgets Company
                              Balance
                               Sheet


         LIABILITIES & EQUITY
         Liabilities:
         Current Liabilities:
                 Accounts Payable                        2,944
                 Notes and Mortgages Payable             1,298
                 Income Taxes Payable                    2,780
                 Accrued Expenses                        27,458
                         Total Current Liabilities       34,480
         Long-Term Debt:
                 Notes and Mortgages Payable             22,423
                 Capital Lease Obligations               44,909
                         Total Long-Term Debt            67,332
         Equity:
                 Common Stock                            50,000
                 Paid-In Capital                         25,000
                 Retained Earnings                       194,586
                         Total Shareholders' Equity      269,586
         TOTAL LIABILITIES & EQUITY                      371,398
```

Figure 14-2: The liabilities as shown on a balance sheet.

Looking at legal aspects

A second very important area to examine is the company's legal obligations. Basically, you want to see copies of all of the Web site's agreements and all other legal documents, including:

- **Lease agreements.** What are the terms of the leases, and when do they terminate? Does the owner want to sell the business because the new lease terms are unfavorable?

- **Marketing agreements.** Many Web sites make their money from advertising instead of e-commerce. Look at the site's advertising and marketing contracts. Are they with stable companies that are likely to remain in business?

- **Domain name registrations.** Does the Web site have clear rights to its domain name? Has another trademark holder challenged it? Is the registration and whois information current? Conduct your own trademark search on the domain name to see if there are any potential conflicts that could cause problems down the road.

✔ **Trademark registration.** If the company has trademarked its domain name or any proprietary products, services, or technology, that can be a big plus for the business.

✔ **Corporate documents.** These include articles of incorporation, bylaws, and ownership percentages.

Have your attorney look over all this information carefully as part of the due diligence process.

Wonder Widgets Company

Fiscal Year Ended December 31, 1999

Revenues	1,796,842
Cost of Goods Sold	1,318,107
Gross Margin	478,735

Operating Expenses:

Selling, General & Administrative	327,482
Depreciation	25,345
Interest on Capitalized Leases	8,774
Interest Expense	1,813
Profit-Sharing Expense	2,393
Total Operating Expenses	365,807

Pretax Income	112,928
Provision for Income Taxes	18,499
Net Income	94,429

Figure 14-3:
An income
statement.

Paying attention to your gut feeling

Intuition is one of the most important factors to consider. How do you feel about the Web site, the owner, the management, and the facilities? Spend some time meeting with the owner face-to-face so that you can gain insights from his or her body language and other subtle clues. Have your friends and colleagues look at the site and give you their honest impressions.

The bottom line is that a Web site has to be a good fit for you as well as a good buy, because it will be consuming a lot of your time, effort, money, and imagination. Make sure that you reach a decision that not only makes good business sense but feels right on an emotional level too.

Considering other factors

In addition to looking at the financial and legal issues involved, you need to take a close look at some other issues as part of your evaluation of a Web site. Some of these are important factors in any type of business, while others are more relevant to Internet-based companies. Your accountant and attorney can give you valuable advice on these considerations.

Content and intellectual property

Make sure that the site's content is deep and up to date. Also, get answers to the following questions:

- ✔ **What are the site's rights and obligations with regard to content and intellectual property? Will they survive a change in ownership?**

- ✔ **How much is the content worth?** Estimate the costs of creating or acquiring that content to obtain a sense of its market value.

Clicks

On the Internet, clicks are directly related to how much advertising and sales a site can generate, because they measure the volume of traffic that the site gets. The most important measurement is the number of *unique visitors* the site attracts — this is equivalent to the number of people who walk into a store. The more people who come through the door, of course, the greater the likelihood of sales.

No matter how many unique visitors the site claims, it is important for you to verify that number for yourself. Work with the seller to use a traffic monitoring program, such as the one offered by Hitbox.com, to verify the site's reported traffic.

Customer base

Almost any successful business — whether in the physical or virtual world — depends on a loyal customer base. Find out if the Web site has a list of registered users or subscribers. If so, what is that list like, and what would it be worth to potential advertisers? Also take a look at customer patterns. Are purchases, for example, seasonal in nature?

Technology

Technology is obviously a key issue with any Internet-based business. You need to evaluate the company's hardware and software capabilities, as well as its storage and Internet access. Get answers to the following questions:

- ✔ Where are the servers kept?
- ✔ Are they maintained by an outside company?
- ✔ Are they maintained in a climate-controlled environment?
- ✔ What is the backup plan?
- ✔ How old is the equipment?
- ✔ What is the history of repairs and maintenance?
- ✔ Where are the servers kept?
- ✔ Are the systems scaleable?

Unless you are a technology expert yourself, hire a technical consultant who can examine all these factors and report back to you on the Web site's technology.

And don't forget . . .

In addition to all these considerations, you should also look into the following matters as part of your due diligence efforts:

- ✔ **Reputation.** Look at the customer history. If customers do repeat business with the site, that's a good sign. Also look at the business's credit history, bank references, Dun & Bradstreet ratings, and any news reports about the online business.

- ✔ **Employees.** Look closely at all contracts, salaries, and other obligations. Talk to each one of the employees to find out how long they have been working there and whether they are happy. Review their resumes. Make sure that the key managers you need will stay around after the sale.

- ✔ **Occupational Safety and Health Administration (OSHA) issues.** These are especially important if warehousing and shipping tasks are part of the business.

- ✔ **Sales tax issues.** If the company is selling products over the Internet, issues surrounding sales tax can be a bit complex in some states.

✔ **Insurance.** Make sure that the online business has adequate coverage, including standard workers' compensation and general liability insurance. Ideally, the site should also have transaction-based sales insurance and additional coverage for Internet-based sales (insuring items such as intellectual property, shipping, and servers).

Coming Up with a Fair Price

If at the end of all your due diligence, you decide that buying the Web site is the move you want to make, the next step is to make an offer on the business. But how do you come up with a fair price? Most likely, you will not have access to the seller's Web site business appraisal, if he or she commissioned one. Therefore, you should consider a range of other factors when trying to come up with a fair offer. You can also use the techniques in Chapter 15 to come up with your own ballpark appraisal of the site.

The key is determining what the company is worth in the marketplace. And this can be a bit tricky to determine, because the Web site resale market is extremely new. But remember that the value of an Internet-based business is a combination of two elements: the worth of the domain name and the value of the business itself. You can start coming up with a fair price by getting a professional appraisal or using the strategies in Chapter 10.

To get an idea of how much the business itself is worth, take these factors into consideration:

✔ **How much would it cost to build this business from scratch?**

✔ **How much did the business make for its previous owners?** A general guideline in the bricks-and-mortar business world is that a fair purchase price is three times a company's net profit per year. This does not necessarily apply in the world of virtual business, where many companies are not yet making any profit, but it can be a good approach to consider.

✔ **How much is it worth to you to own the Web site?** This is a very subjective matter, and it has a lot to do with what you plan to use the Web site for. Like a gut feeling, it is a personal but very important factor.

✔ **What is it worth to you to eliminate the competition, if that is why you want to buy the site?**

✔ **How much is it worth to acquire the site's content or traffic?**

✔ **What is it worth to acquire its employees and strategic relationships?**

The fact is that there is no textbook way to come up with a fair offer for a Web site. By considering these questions, you can get some realistic sense of where to start and, most importantly, what the site would be worth to you.

Closing the Deal

When you have made your offer, the next step, of course, is to negotiate with the seller until you have arrived at a price that is acceptable to both of you. At this point, with the help of your attorney and accountant, you should move into the final phase of the transaction, which includes:

✔ Writing and signing a letter of agreement, stating all the details of the deal as simply and straightforwardly as possible, in layman's terms

✔ Arranging financing

✔ Meeting all the closing conditions

✔ Completing the Web site purchase

Obviously, buying a Web site is far more complicated than buying a domain name. It can be costly, too. In addition to the purchase price for the site, you have to pay the fees of your attorney and accountant and possibly one or more other consultants. It can be well worth it, however, if the site is right for you. And who knows? It may position you to benefit from the future growth and dramatic opportunities of the Internet.

When you start this process, it is important to remember that only a fraction of the letters of intent actually end up as a successful deal. You have to clear a lot of hurdles before you reach the closing stage, and both you and the seller may have many opportunities to back out, depending on the terms of your agreement.

The process of buying any business — including a Web site — is rarely quick and smooth. It often takes much longer and is more expensive than you imagine.

Chapter 15

Valuing a Web Site

• •

• •

*I*f you own and operate a Web-based business and are interested in selling it or raising more capital to invest in developing it further, you need to know the value of that online enterprise. Knowing the value is the only way that you can price it accurately or give potential investors a clear sense of the enterprise's worth.

But the fact is that appraising an Internet business can be a difficult task. Many Web sites, especially those featuring fast, efficient business solutions, may have seen their value increase rapidly and dramatically in the early days of the dot-com revolution, only to see the values plunge just as dramatically when the market began shying away from Web-based businesses. Complicating the picture is the fact that a lot of Web sites are not yet making a profit. Many, in fact, have been losing money. Nevertheless, if a Web-based company can survive the early ups and downs of the Internet marketplace with a successful product or service, its value, growth, and earning could eventually skyrocket.

Online businesses at the high end of the market have been able to appraise their sites with the help of highly priced investment bankers, backed by teams of analysts. Until now, however, Web-based businesses at the middle and lower ranks of the marketplace have had no readily available appraisal option or methodology that they could apply themselves.

Now, however, there is such an alternative. GreatDomains.com's division, GreatWebsites.com, has created a brand-new proprietary valuation methodology (patent pending) that takes into account both traditional and nontraditional measures for valuing Internet-based companies. In this chapter, we look at the basic framework of this approach and explore ways that you can obtain a professional Web site appraisal or develop your own ballpark estimate of your Web-based business's worth.

Note: References to these proprietary methodologies should not be construed as a license to use, make, or sell products or services that may be covered under these proprietary methodologies. The consent of GreatDomains.com should be obtained prior to any commercial use thereof.

Identifying the Keys to a Web Site's Value

Of course, many circumstances affect a Web site's value, most of which are beyond anyone's control. The Web site market is, after all, brand-new and subject to rapidly changing forces. Nevertheless, there are two key components that essentially make up the value of any Web-based business:

- The domain name
- The Internet business itself

In the following sections, we take a closer look at each of these key elements.

The value of the domain name

Your Web enterprise's domain name is like the land your business is located on. As a result, the more valuable your domain name, the more valuable your business may be. Of course, the opposite is true as well — the lower the value of your domain name, the lower the overall value of your Web-based business.

In Chapter 10, we explore in detail all the factors that go into assessing the value of a domain name. In brief, those elements include:

- **The number of characters.** Typically, short names are better than long names, because they are usually easier to remember and spell.
- **Commerce.** A domain name's value is mainly determined by its ability to deliver traffic and revenue to a business. There are a number of factors to consider when appraising a domain name's commercial value:

  - The utility of the domain name to a business

  - The size of the most relevant industry

  - The domain name's relevance to e-commerce

  - The degree to which it is rare or generic

  - The number of companies likely to desire the domain name

  - Its potential for use as a brand name in e-commerce

✔ **The TLD.** Some extensions are more valuable than others. Currently, the `.com` TLD is perceived as the most valuable category of Internet address. Second is `.net` (along with some new TLDs such as `.tv` and `.cc`), and third in value is `.org`.

By weighing all these factors according to the methodology in Chapter 10, you can come up with a ballpark estimate of your domain name's value.

The value of the Internet business

The second element in determining a Web site's value is performing a separate appraisal of the Web-based business itself. We explore a basic approach that you can use to assess your business's value in the "Valuing a Web-Based Business" section later in this chapter.

Adding it all up

When you have determined the value of the business, you need to balance it with the value of the domain name. They influence each other, and, in many cases, the value of one or the other will be greater. There are, in fact, four different weighting possibilities, based on GreatDomains.com's patent-pending proprietary model:

✔ **Strong domain name and weak online business.** A good domain name is one of the basic building blocks of a successful online business. Most consumers feel overwhelmed when searching for goods or services on the Internet, and one way to attract and keep them is by giving them an easy Internet address to remember. However, the value of this asset is undermined if the surrounding business is not performing well. Businesses that fall in this category need to invest in the company in order to capitalize on their strong domain name.

✔ **Strong domain name and strong online business.** This, of course, is the best of all worlds. A Web site has maximum value when it has a strong Internet-based business to capitalize on a strong domain name, which, in turn, drives traffic, helps build revenue, and enhances brand equity. When companies capitalize on their strong domain name, the value of their business rises.

✔ **Weak domain name and weak online business.** This is the worst of the possible scenarios. Basically, in this part of the grid, businesses are struggling to drive traffic to their site. To do this, they are spending money that could be better allocated to their operations. Companies that fall into this category should look at investing in a new domain name to begin the process of building a stronger online presence.

✓ **Weak domain name and strong online business.** Surprisingly enough, there are companies that fall into this category. If you have a strong business concept but a weak domain name, you may have to spend a lot of money to make customers aware of your location on the Web. Like a great business in an out-of-the-way neighborhood, companies that fall into this category must spend a great deal of money to drive traffic to their site.

You cannot just add the value of your domain name to your business value to get an accurate valuation of your Web site. If you have a strong domain name and a weak online enterprise, for example, the value of your domain name may be more important and your most valuable business asset. On the other hand, if you have a strong business as well as a strong domain name, the value of your domain name may not add much to your total appraisal. That is because it is probably already contributing to the value of your site by bringing in a significant level of traffic.

The point to remember is that you have to take both of these elements — your domain name and your business's value — into consideration, even though the balance between them may vary from site to site.

Valuing a Web-Based Business

Valuing any business can be a challenging task. Some methods predict future revenues and cash flows, and then adjust those projections based on the current marketplace to come up with a plausible estimate. That is a difficult model to use for Web-based businesses, however, because many of them are not making any profit, while others are seeing their revenues increase rapidly. Both situations make predicting future revenues and cash flows very difficult.

Another common method for valuing a company is the *comparable sales method*. This method presents problems for Internet-based companies as well. With this model, as with real estate, appraisers try to find recently sold companies whose sales characteristics — such as size, market share, and revenues — closely match that of the business they are trying to appraise. Because the Internet industry is so young, however, little sales data exists, so this method is not a useful model.

One approach that does make sense, however, is the *comparable company analysis*. In this model, you use financial and non-financial measures of publicly traded companies to get an indication of value. In effect, it enables you to estimate the value that the market would place on your Internet-based business if it were traded publicly. This, at present, may be the most effective way to estimate the value of an Internet-based business. We cover this approach in the following sections.

Step 1: Analyzing your underlying business

Before you can identify a comparable company, you need to have as clear a picture as possible of your own online business. A good place to start is by answering these questions:

✔ **What type of Web site do you have?** There are several different kinds of Web-based businesses, including:

- **E-commerce sites,** on which customers perform purchasing transactions.

- **Portals,** which draw traffic by assembling a broad range of Web links and content for visitors, such as Yahoo.com, About.com, Autoweb.com, and America Online.

- **Branding and informational sites,** which serve mainly as a promotional vehicle for your company's products and services — like an online billboard or brochure — without the transactional functions of an e-commerce site.

Many sites combine one or more of these online strategies.

✔ **What is the purpose of your site?** Think specifically about your immediate business goals. For example, are you trying to:

- Sell used books

- Provide searchable information on political candidates

- Create a portal dedicated to information about dogs

- Attract customers with deep content, then direct them to your offline services

✔ **What are you selling?** Is it, for example, hard-to-find old record albums, travel reservations, knitting accessories, subscriptions to content, offline services, or traffic?

✔ **Who are your customers?** This can be a difficult question to answer unless you have a registration or subscription function on your site.

✔ **Do you have any proprietary features, such as technology that you have created or trademarked brands?**

✔ **What customers does your Web site target?** What types of consumers are you trying to reach? Homeowners between the ages of 40 and 60? Business travelers? Model train hobbyists?

✔ **Who are your competitors?** What other sites offer similar services or products to your target customers?

✔ **What is your current position in the market?** How do you rank compared to your competitors? If you sell new books online, for example, your business may be dwarfed by Amazon.com. But if you have a small business selling sought-after rock-and-roll T-shirts on the Web, you may be the leader in your marketplace.

✔ **What separates your company from competitors?** Is there anything you offer that adds special, unique value for your customers?

After you have answered these basic questions about your Web-based business, the next step is to gather the following financial information about your site's performance over the last three months:

✔ **Revenues.** How much money did your site bring in over the past year? Determine how much was generated by the following:

- **Advertising.** How much of your revenue was generated by sales of advertising placements on your site?

- **E-commerce.** How much money came from online sales of products or services?

- **Sponsorships.** How much revenue did you earn through co-branding or sponsorship deals, such as the placement of a sponsor's name or logo on your site?

- **Subscriptions.** How much money did you make from paid subscriptions or registrations to access certain content or services?

✔ **Expenses.** How much did your business spend to generate those revenues? Expenses may include:

- **Technology costs, such as servers and Internet access**

- **Advertising**

- **Marketing**

- **Shipping**

- **Research and development, such as programming expenses**

- **General administration, rent, computer leases, and furniture**

- **Salaries and compensation**

✔ **Purchase offers.** Has anyone made an offer to buy your Web site? If so, how much did they bid for it?

✔ **Site statistics.** You can build the world's greatest site, but if you do not have any traffic, the site will not have much commercial value. You need to know what your traffic was for the last three months — and whether it was increasing, decreasing, or staying at a relatively constant level. From your Web hosting provider, find out what your monthly totals are, for each of the last three months, in the following categories:

> • **Unique visitors:** Separate individuals who visited your site
>
> • **Page views:** The number of pages visited
>
> • **Average user's session length:** On a weekly, hourly, or daily basis.

Step 2: Finding comparable companies

When you have assembled all the information in Step 1, the next step is to identify a publicly traded company that shares the same business emphasis as yours. For example, if you have an e-commerce Web site that features deep content on the subject of aquariums and sells aquarium-related products over the Web, you look for comparable public companies that are engaged in similar activities.

Chances are slim, however, that you will find a public company that specializes in online sales of aquarium-related products. Your best bet, then, is to identify a number of publicly traded companies that use the closest possible business model.

Some companies that you may consider for the purpose of this valuation process could be:

✔ **Buy.com:** A site that sells computers, software, books, golf gear, CDs, DVDs, consumer electronics, and games. Buy.com is the one of the biggest retailers on the Internet.

✔ **Outpost.com:** An Internet retailer of computer hardware, software, and accessories to the consumer and small office marketplace. This online store offers over 160,000 products, many of which are available to customers via electronic software download.

✔ **CNET.com:** A Web site that offers information on the Internet, computers, and technology to buyers, sellers, and suppliers all over the world.

✔ **Amazon.com:** An online company that offers millions of books, as well as CDs, DVDs, videos, toys, tools, and electronics.

Find at least three companies for the purpose of your comparison.

Step 3: Researching the comparable companies

The next phase of the valuation process is to obtain some key financial information about the public companies that you have identified. You can easily access this information online. First, you need to find out the revenues of each company for the most recent 12-month period. Then you need to determine each company's current market capitalization. In this section, we let you know how you can do this.

Determining annual revenues

To find out each company's revenues for the past 12 months, you can go to one of many financial Web sites, such as:

- ✔ **CBS MarketWatch** (cbs.marketwatch.com)
- ✔ **CNBC.com** (www.cnbc.com)
- ✔ **FreeEDGAR** (www.freeedgar.com)
- ✔ **Morningstar** (www.morningstar.com)

As an example, let's say you're interested in finding the revenues for the past 12 months for Buy.com. We'll use FreeEDGAR as an example of a site you can use to do this research. Here's how you do it:

1. **Go to** www.freeedgar.com.

2. **In the Company Name box, type in "Buy" (short for Buy.com)**

3. **Click the Search button.**

4. **Under the listing Buy Com Inc, click on View Filings.**

On the same line, you will also see the link SIC Code: 5734. *SIC* stands for Standard Industrial Classification. By clicking on that code number, you see a list of many companies that are similar in various ways to Buy.com. You can potentially find more comparable companies for your valuation process by exploring those sites and identifying online businesses whose business models are similar to yours.

5. **To determine Buy.com's annual revenue, look at its *10-Q statements,* or quarterly reports.**

Start by clicking on the first 10-Q in the list.

6. **On the left side of the screen, you see a separate scroll bar. Scroll down under Table of Contents and click on Income Statement.**

7. **On the Net Revenues line, look at the column titled Nine Months Ended September 30, 2000 (see Figure 15-1).**

The number you see is $590,965,000 (the listed number $590,965 is in thousands). This gives you total revenues for the last nine months. Next, you need to find the company's revenues for the prior three-month period — ending December 31, 1999 — to determine the company's revenues for the past 12 months.

8. **Click the Back button on your browser twice to return to the screen listing the various financial statements that you saw in Step 5.**

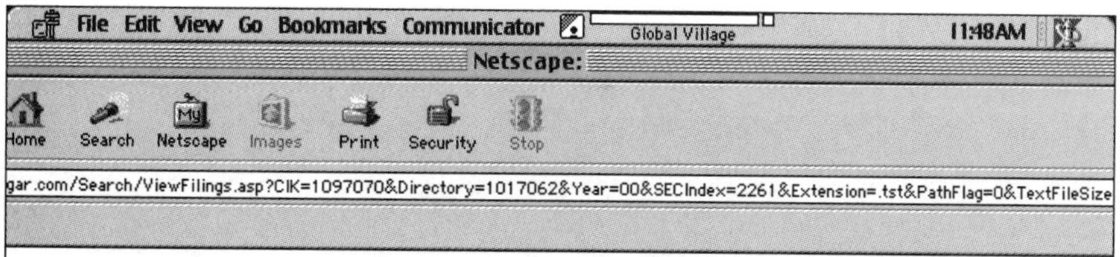

	Quarter Ended September 30,		Nine Months Ended September 30,	
	2000	1999	2000	1999
Net revenues	$ 190,150	$ 158,960	$ 590,965	$ 396,172
Cost of goods sold	177,437	159,094	557,622	401,426
Gross profit (loss)	12,713	(134)	33,343	(5,254)
Operating expenses:				
Sales and marketing	21,229	15,560	67,768	42,453
Product development	7,097	1,795	17,252	3,851
General and administrative	6,642	5,293	20,263	12,875
Depreciation	1,176	357	3,539	702
Amortization of goodwill and other intangibles	3,237	831	9,050	2,307
Amortization of deferred compensation and warrants	660	8,467	2,542	12,438
Total operating expenses	40,041	32,303	120,414	74,626
Operating loss	(27,328)	(32,437)	(87,071)	(79,880)
Other income (expense):				
Interest income (expense)	2,015	(796)	5,715	(721)
Other	30	49	(792)	74
Total other income (expense)	2,045	(747)	4,923	(647)
Net loss before equity in losses of joint ventures	(25,283)	(33,184)	(82,148)	(80,527)

Figure 15-1: The Buy.com Income statement.

Screenshot courtesy of EDGAR Online, Inc.

9. **Click on the "S1-A" filing for 2/7/2000.**
10. **On the left side of the screen, click on Body.**
11. **Scroll down to the table titled Three Months Ended and look at the Net Revenues figure for the three months that ended on December 31, 1999 (see Figure 15-2).**

    That number is $200,676,000.
12. **Add that figure to the nine-month revenue number of $590,965,000 for a 12-month revenue total of $791,641,000.**

Determining the company's market capitalization

The next step is to find out the market capitalization figure for that public company. You can do this easily by going to one of the financial Web sites such as:

- **CBS MarketWatch** (`cbs.marketwatch.com`)
- **CNBC.com** (`www.cnbc.com`)

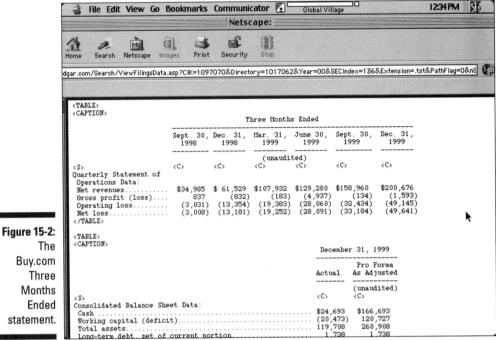

Figure 15-2:
The
Buy.com
Three
Months
Ended
statement.

Screenshot courtesy of EDGAR Online, Inc.

Here we take a look at how to determine Buy.com's market capitalization step-by-step, using CBS MarketWatch.

1. **Go to** `cbs.marketwatch.com`.

2. **On the left side of the screen, enter the stock symbol for Buy.com, which is BUYX, and then click on the arrow.**

   If you do not know the stock symbol of the company you are researching, click on Symbol Lookup.

3. **On the left side of the screen, click on Fundamentals.**

   Under Fundamentals for Buy Com Inc, the third line down says "Market Cap: 192.7 million" (see Figure 15-3). This means that the market capitalization for that public company is $192,700,000.

When you know the company's annual revenues and its market capitalization, you can easily determine its market cap multiple — the number that will help you assess your own company's value. To do this:

1. **Divide the market capitalization figure by the annual revenues.**

   In the case of Buy.com, you would divide the market capitalization number of $192,700,000 by its annual revenues of $791,641,000.

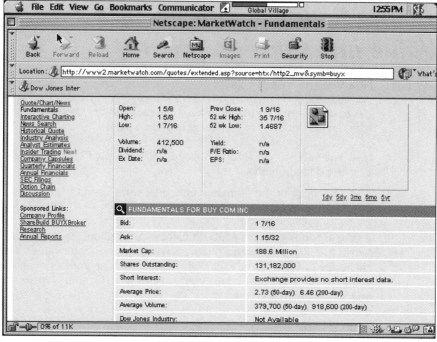

Figure 15-3:
The
Buy.com
Funda-
mentals.

Screenshot courtesy of CBS MarketWatch

2. **Your total is the market cap multiple.**

   For Buy.com, the multiple in this case is 0.24.

Step 4: Applying the market cap multiple to your company

To get a ballpark estimate of the value of your company in today's marketplace, take the multiples of all your comparable companies, average them, and apply that average number to the annual revenues of your own online business.

For example, if the average market cap multiple of all the companies you are researching is 0.32, and the annual revenues of your Web site total $1,000,000, you would do this simple math to get a ballpark value estimate:

$1,000,000 \times 0.32 = $320,000

Taking Your Domain Name's Value into Consideration

Now that you have the value of your domain name and the value of your online business, you can come up with a total ballpark value for your Web-based company. The estimated total value of your company is equal to whichever is greater of the following two values:

- ✔ The value of the Internet-based business, plus some possible credit for the domain name
- ✔ The value of the domain name, plus some credit for the Web-based business

If your business is worth $320,000, for example, and your domain name is worth $10,000, your entire business would probably be valued somewhere in the range of $300,000 to $325,000. That is because your domain name's value probably already factors into your business performance in some manner — and staying on the conservative side when you are making a valuation estimate is wise.

On the other hand, if you have a very strong domain name — worth, for example, $950,000 — and your business itself is worth about $320,000, the total value of your Web site might be around $1 million. After all, the most valuable part of your business is the domain name — and it may in fact be responsible for much of your business performance. As a result, you should not add much of a premium for the business itself.

Being Aware of Other Factors That Can Add Value to Your Business

Valuing a Web site is a fairly subjective process, but it can give you some useful benchmarks when you are trying to assess the value of your own site. Your online business may also have some additional value if:

- ✔ **It is already making a profit.** This suggests that you have a good business model and are managing your expenses well.
- ✔ **Someone has made an offer to buy your site.** This indicates that some feature of your business is especially attractive to the marketplace
- ✔ **Your site has a significant number of unique visitors and page views.** If visitors are spending considerable time exploring your Web site, that may make your business more appealing to advertisers as well as potential purchasers.

Hire a pro

The methodology we outline in this chapter is a very simplified approach that can give you a very basic, ballpark valuation estimate. For the most accurate results, however, you should commission a professional valuation by experienced experts using much more sophisticated methodologies.

As the Web site resale market matures, more and more companies will likely be offering professional valuation services. Currently, you can have your Web site affordably appraised by contacting GreatWebsites.com at www. greatwebsites.com.

Chapter 16

Selling Your Web-Based Business

*I*f you own a Web-based business, you have been part of an exciting and historic phenomenon, the birth of a brand new industry. Like any revolutionary idea, online business has had — and will probably continue to have — its ups and downs, thrilling gains and frustrating disappointments. Whether or not you choose to go the distance with your Web enterprise — riding out all the changes and challenges of a growing industry — is a question that only you can answer.

If you do not want to make a long-term commitment to your Web business, you may decide that trying to sell it is an attractive option. Given the fact that Internet business is a brand-new industry, however, you need to consider many issues before you put your Web site up for sale.

In this chapter, we explore some of the challenges of the new Web site resale market. We also fill you in on the steps you need to take to find a buyer for your Web-based business.

Determining Whether You Should Sell

If you've built a Web-based business, you've invested not just money but a lot of personal capital as well, including time, creativity, plans, and expectations. As a result, the idea of putting that Web site on the market can be an emotional decision. But it may be one of the options to consider if you're a Web business owner who is:

✔ **Tired of maintaining your Web enterprise.** If you no longer have a strong interest in your site, your business may suffer if you continue to operate it.

✔ **Experiencing changed circumstances.** Factors such as illness, death, divorce, or new commitments can affect the amount of time that you have to give to your business, which in turn could make the business suffer.

✔ **Hoping to cash in on your business assets.** Even if your site is not producing much in the way of profit, the site may be worth a significant amount of money to someone else. By putting your Web business up for sale, you may be able to turn that Internet asset into cash.

✔ **Hoping to help your Web enterprise grow.** You may have reached the limits of growth with your current resources. By selling your Web site to a larger company, you may be able to help your Web-based business achieve its growth potential.

No matter what your reasons for selling may be, the same words of advice hold true — the Web site market is not yet delivering quick riches. The fact is that it can take many months, or even years, before a Web-based business sells — if it sells at all.

However, keep in mind that the marketplace is young. Over time, maybe six months or a year, the market may become much more active, increasing your odds of successfully selling your site for a fair price. Until that time, however, you may want to wait while you work to increase your site's marketability.

If, on the other hand, you do decide to plunge ahead into the Web site marketplace, read on to find out what you need to know.

Step #1: Getting an Appraisal

Owners of traditional bricks-and-mortar businesses often do not know the true value of their enterprise. But the same can be true for owners of Web-based businesses. When you're operating in a brand-new marketplace, with few sales of comparable companies to look to as examples, assessing how much a Web enterprise is worth can be baffling, especially if the Web business is making little or no money yet.

Before you decide whether to proceed with putting your Web site on the market, have it professionally valued by an appraisal service, such as GreatWebsites.com (www.greatwebsites.com). The range of value that the appraiser comes up with will give you important information for figuring out your pricing and negotiating strategy.

You can get a ballpark sense of your site's value by following the do-it-yourself instructions in Chapter 15. But if you are serious about putting your Web business up for sale, a professional valuation is probably well worth the investment.

Step #2: Looking for a Buyer

After you've determined the value of your business, the next step is to begin the long process of looking for the right purchaser. You can do this in several ways:

✔ **Work with an investment bank.** These professionals help bring buyers and sellers together for large, high-end transactions.

✔ **Work with a business broker.** Small, traditional companies often use business brokers to facilitate a sale. If your Web business has a significant bricks-and-mortar component, using a business broker may be an option.

✔ **List your site with online brokers.** A few brokers on the Internet specialize in Web site listings. As the market matures, many will offer an increasing variety of features and services.

Online Web site listing services include:

- Axiopolis (www.axiopolis.com)
- GreatWebsites.com (www.greatwebsites.com)
- Time2Sell (www.time2sell.com)
- WebSites-4-Sale (www.websites-4-sale.net)
- WebSiteBroker.com (www.websitebroker.com)

✔ **Do it yourself.** Given the fact that the Web site resale market is so young, your best strategy may be to list your business with an online broker while actively looking for a buyer yourself. There are a number of strategies you can use for researching potential buyers, including the following:

- **Search the Web:** The most promising and direct way to find a likely buyer may be to surf the Web looking for companies that could benefit from the customers, services, products, proprietary information, or technology that your Web-based business offers.

  For example, if your site, 123Widgets.com, is a successful resale broker for previously owned widgets, it may be an attractive acquisition for a retail site specializing in the sale of new widgets to consumers. By adding your features and offering a broader scope of services, the acquiring company may be able to expand its market. The key is to find a company whose business would be complemented and enhanced by the purchase of your site.

- **Talk to others in the industry:** Individuals who know the players in your market — such as vendors, contractors, or suppliers — may be able to give you valuable insight and advice about potential purchasers. Trade associations can also be a good source of information.

Step #3: Making Contact with Potential Prospects

When you have identified a company that you think may be interested in purchasing your Web site, the next step is to obtain contact information for the decision-maker in charge of business development, strategic planning, or strategic development, or the Chief Financial Officer (CFO) of the company.

You may be able to find some initial contact information on the company's Web site. If the business is publicly traded, you can obtain information at Hoovers Online (hoovers.com), a subscription site that lists all public companies and their officers. (If you join Hoovers Online, you can do a site search for a company's name, then click on "Officers" to get a list of key individuals.)

Generally speaking, it's a good idea to make the first contact with a decision-maker at the lowest levels of a business, and then work your way up as you get more feedback and gather more information.

Sending a letter

When you have the contact information you need, put together a cover letter that describes your business and the opportunity that it offers the potential buyer. Talk about:

- ✔ What your business brings to the table
- ✔ The unique qualities of your business that complement the company you are contacting
- ✔ How your business can help the potential purchaser expand or better serve its customer base

The key point to get across is this: What would the purchasing company gain by acquiring your site?

Following up by phone

A week or so after you have mailed your introductory letter, contact the individual you sent it to by phone and ask to set up a face-to-face meeting to discuss your proposition in detail.

In most cases, when you ask for a face-to-face meeting, the answer is likely to be "no." Many companies are frequently approached by sellers. As a result, they may be skeptical about the value of the opportunity that you're offering. Even if your first contact gives you the brush-off, don't give up. Contact another decision maker at a higher level, until you get a final "no thanks" — or a thumbs-up to continue.

Step #4: Setting Up a Meeting

If you do succeed in interesting a buyer, a face-to-face meeting is your best — and perhaps only — opportunity to make the sale. So if you get someone at the company to agree to meet with you, make the most of it. Prepare for this meeting carefully and be ready to make an investment of time and money to put the best possible face on your Web business.

Even if you run your Web-based business out a spare bedroom or garage, you need to present your business as professionally as possible. Travel to the potential purchaser's headquarters, if necessary, for the meeting. Put together a polished presentation. Prepare key documents that you will need to make your case, including a business profile that describes:

- How your business started and its history to date
- How it operates
- How it makes money
- How it markets its products or services
- Unique proprietary features, such as content or technology
- Your company's competitive position
- Employee information
- Key suppliers and contractors

Prepare statements showing your business's financial results, including:

- **Balance sheet, listing all of your company's financial assets and liabilities**
- **Income statement, showing your site's revenues and expenses over a specific period of time**
- **Cash flow statement**
- **Statement showing percentages of ownership in your Web business**

In addition to financial results, prepare financial projections of your business's future performance, including:

- ✔ An income statement projecting results for the next three to five years
- ✔ The amount of cash your business will need to achieve those projected results
- ✔ How many employees the business will need
- ✔ At what point your Web business will break even financially

Be sure to document the assumptions and historical results on which you are basing your projections. Provide information on:

- ✔ The size of your market
- ✔ The revenue potential of your company
- ✔ The market share you are aiming for
- ✔ How you plan to gain this share of the market
- ✔ Your company's history of growth
- ✔ Your company's growth in traffic, including the number of unique visitors and page views
- ✔ The number of visitors who actually buy products or services from your business, and the change in that number over time

Step #5: Negotiating the Price

If your presentation successfully convinces the potential purchaser to buy your Web site, the next step is to negotiate and agree on a sales price. The professional valuation you obtain at the beginning of the selling process should give you a basic range of value for planning your negotiating strategy.

At this point, if you don't have a financial background or experience with complex business transactions, using the services of experienced business advisors, such as an attorney and accountant, to help you negotiate and structure the sale would be wise.

Step #6: Closing the Deal

Because business sales are complex and can often involve government regulations, rely on your attorney and accountant to facilitate the final phases of the deal.

Meanwhile, there are a number of tips that you should keep in mind:

- ✔ **Put everything in writing.** There is no such thing as a gentleman's agreement when it comes to selling a Web-based business (or any business, for that matter). Put all the financial points in writing so that there will be no room for dispute later.

- ✔ **Get the best possible advice.** Paying for the most experienced, competent advisors is well worth the investment. If you don't get good advice during the sale, it may cost you much more than you would have paid to obtain the best possible legal and financial counsel.

- ✔ **Keep it quiet.** If people know that you are planning to sell your site, they may act in ways that may undermine your business. Employees could get nervous and look for other jobs, and customers may start to drift away. As a result, keeping your sale plans under wraps until the deal is final is always a good idea.

- ✔ **Be prepared.** At all stages of a prospective business sale, it is important for you to be as well prepared as possible. It is all too easy to blow the deal, and — especially in the Web-based business market — you may not get another shot. Treat each opportunity like your only chance to sell your site — because it may very well be.

Figuring Out What to Do If You Can't Find a Buyer

If all your efforts to sell your site have left you empty-handed, the truth is that you probably have lots of company. Because the market is so young, many Web-business owners may find this an extraordinarily difficult time to sell.

If you can't find a seller, ask yourself the following questions:

- ✔ **Do you want to keep running your business?** Do you have enough interest and energy left to continue to operate and grow your business site?

- ✔ **Do you want to shut it down?** If you are really ready to move on, closing down the business may be a serious consideration.

- ✔ **Do you want to develop the business and make it more marketable?** This may be the most promising option, if you have the wherewithal to continue. By increasing your traffic and unique, proprietary features, you can make your business more valuable and attractive to potential purchasers in the future — when the Web-business market has matured and you may have a better competitive position.

Part VII

The Part of Tens

The 5th Wave — By Rich Tennant

NO INTERNET ADDRESS

PLEASE

In this part . . .

This wouldn't be a *For Dummies* book without a Part of Tens. Here you'll find quick bursts of trivia as well as advice you can use in the real world of buying and selling domain names. We give you the top prices paid for domain names, so you have something to shoot for when you enter this ever-changing marketplace. And we let you know about some common mistakes you should try to avoid when you're buying, selling, or registering a domain name. Read on!

Chapter 17

The Top Ten Prices Paid for Domain Names

- -

In This Chapter

▶ Five domain names that sold for more than $3 million

▶ Five domain names that sold for $1 to $2 million

- -

Although the average domain name sells for around $7,000, there have been many high-profile sales in the million-dollar-and-above category. Here are the top ten domain name sale prices, based on publicly available information.

Business.com, $ 7.5 million

In December 1999, Houston entrepreneur Marc Ostrofsky sold the Business.com domain name to Ecompanies for $7.5 million, a figure far and above all previous domain name sales.

Korea.com, $5 million

In March 2000, Korea Thrunet Co., Ltd., a data communications services provider in Korea, acquired the Korea.com domain name for the price of $5 million.

AltaVista.com, $3.35 million

In 1998 Compaq Computer bought the AltaVista.com domain name for $3.35 million from the owner of a software company in San Jose, California.

Loans.com, $3 million

In January 2000, Marcelo Siero, an engineer in northern California, sold the domain name Loans.com to financial giant Bank of America for $3 million. In 1994, Siero had registered the domain name for free.

Wine.com, $3 million

In September 1999, VirtualVineyard.com — an Internet wine seller — paid $3 million to purchase the domain name Wine.com from David Harmon, the owner of a helicopter tour business in California's Napa Valley.

Autos.com, $2.2 million

In December 1999, CarsDirect.com — an Internet-based auto dealer — paid $2.2 million in cash to purchase the Autos.com domain name from the Atlanta-based Britt Corp. company.

Express.com, $2 million

In December 1999, DVD EXPRESS bought the domain name Express.com for $2 million.

Wallstreet.com, $1.03 million

In April 1999, former Albuquerque stockbroker Eric Wade and his two partners sold their domain name WallStreet.com to the Venezuelan company Players Only for $1.03 million.

If.com, $1 million

In May 2000, Halifax plc., a British company, bought the domain name If.com for $1 million for its Intelligent Finance division.

Beauty.cc, $1 million

In June 2000, David Sams — whose company, David Sams Industries, markets the .cc country-code TLD — sold Beauty.cc for $1 million to domain name trader Universal Domains. It was the top price ever paid for a domain name without the .com TLD.

Chapter 18

Ten Great Domain Name Web Sites

*W*hether you are looking for information on registering, trademarking, buying, or selling a domain name, these are ten of the top sites to head for. You'll also find a wealth of information, resources, and links to news, articles, opinion, and predictions about the fast-growing domain name marketplace at the URLs featured below, ranked according to the number of unique visitors they attract.

Domain Name News

www.nvo.com/dnnews/home

Domain Name News is an all-around resource for news and information about domain names. The site has links to recent domain name news articles, information about domain name buying and selling, and resources on domain name trademark law and a wide variety of issues.

GreatDomains.com

www.greatdomains.com

GreatDomains.com offers the leading marketplace for buying and selling domain names. The site also features services such as escrow and domain name and Web site valuations.

IANA

www.iana.org

IANA, the Internet Assigned Numbers Authority, provides links to lists of all generic and country-code TLDs, with administrative contact information for each of the various extensions.

ICANN

www.icann.org

ICANN, the Internet Corporation for Assigned Names and Numbers, is the international administrator for Internet domain names. This site provides administrative and technical information on topics such as domain name registration (including lists of all ICANN-approved registrars), and domain name dispute resolution.

idNames

www.idnames.com

idNames enables you to check domain name availability and register names instantly for more than fifty unrestricted ccTLDs worldwide, It also provides detailed international whois information on domain name availability in 192 different countries.

Melbourne IT

www.melbourneit.com

The world's second largest domain name registrar — and the largest in the Asia Pacific region — Melbourne IT permits you to search and register domain names in Chinese, Japanese, and Korean characters.

Network Solutions, Inc.

www.networksolutions.com

Network Solutions, a subsidiary of VeriSign, Inc., was the first company to serve as a domain name registrar. The site offers many features, including domain name registration, Web site and e-commerce tools, e-mail services, and domain name statistics.

U.S. Patent and Trademark Office

www.uspto.gov

The United States Patent and Trademark Office Web site offers a wealth of information on the domain name trademark process, as well as tools for filing for federal trademarks online.

VeriSign Global Registry Services

www.verisign-grs.com

As the organization that maintains the definitive directory of all .com, .net, and .org Web addresses, VeriSign Global Registry Services permits you to do the most accurate possible whois search of all registered domain names for those gTLDs.

Web Marketing Info Center

www.wilsonweb.com/webmarket/domain.htm

Web Marketing Info Center has a domain name section with links to dozens of articles and resources related to domain names. The site, created by Wilson Internet, also features sections on other Web- and Internet-related topics.

Chapter 19

Ten Mistakes to Avoid When Registering a Domain Name

In This Chapter

▶ Getting tips for registering the best possible domain name

▶ Finding advice for preventing big domain name problems

*I*f you're ready to jump into the domain name game and register a domain name of your own, consider this list of don'ts before you start. We've put together the top pitfalls that people often stumble into when they select and acquire an Internet address. By avoiding these common problems, you'll avoid a lot of domain name headaches down the road.

Registering a Difficult-to-Spell Name

Here's a general guideline for almost every domain name: Make sure it's easy to spell. No matter how much people may want to find your site, they will have a hard time if your domain name is something tough to spell like Zzyphthix.com. The harder a name is to spell, the greater the chance that customers will not be able to find it — and they will end up doing business with someone else.

Registering a Name That's Hard to Remember

A domain name that has ten characters or less is an ideal length, because it's easy for people to remember. Twelve or even fifteen characters are usually fine, too. Just keep in mind that the longer the domain name is, the harder it is to remember. Complex or obscure domain names — like 2hrspxyc-inc.com —

can be also extremely hard for people to recall. On the other hand, a domain name that is "top of mind," like Loans.com or Cars.com will likely generate more traffic, because people don't have to struggle to remember them.

Registering a Name That Infringes on Someone Else's Trademark

Trademark owners often take legal action against people who infringe on their trademark rights. As a result, you need to be sure to choose a business domain name that does not conflict with anyone else's trademark.

Ignorance is no protection in the eyes of the law. Even if you had no clue that the domain name you registered and have been using is infringing on another's mark, you may end up losing it — and that can be a serious blow to your business.

Neglecting to Conduct a Trademark Search of the Name You Register

To protect yourself from potential trademark problems, be sure to conduct some trademark research as soon as you register your domain name and before you use it in commerce. Performing this due diligence is your responsibility. Failing to do so can be used as evidence to support a claim that you deliberately infringed on another's mark.

Forgetting to Renew Your Registration

If you forget to renew your domain name registration, your rights to the name will lapse. If you later try to sell the name, you may find that you are selling something that no longer belongs to you.

Renewing your domain name is usually a simple matter. Some registrars will contact you with a reminder several weeks before your domain name registration expires; other registrars, however, require you to keep track of your own renewal deadlines. In most cases, you can follow the instructions that your registrar provides to renew your registration quickly and easily online.

Neglecting to Update Your whois Registration Information

Always make sure that your contact information in the whois domain name registration database is up-to-date. If you move or change your e-mail address and do not update whois, a potential buyer will not be able to locate you and make an offer to purchase your domain name.

Registering a Name That's Offensive in Another Language

The Internet is a global environment. Especially if you will be marketing your products or services overseas, be sure to check the meaning of your domain name with native foreign language speakers to make sure that they are not offensive to non-English-speaking audiences.

Not Registering Common Misspellings

Be sure to register misspellings of your domain name. If you don't, and if you have a successful Web site, a competitor may register common misspellings of your domain name and divert poor spellers and other potential customers from your site.

Not Listing Yourself as the Administrative Contact

Make sure that when you register your domain name, you list yourself — not your Web hosting provider or ISP — as the administrative contact. This is crucial, because the administrative contact generally has the power to approve or prevent the transfer of the name. If you want to sell your domain name at a later date and neglect to list yourself as the administrative contact, you could run into some serious problems.

Not Acting Quickly to Register a Domain Name That You Like

If you find an available domain name that you like, register it right away. With thousands of domain names being registered every day, you can be sure that a good domain name won't be available for very long.

Chapter 20

Ten Mistakes to Avoid When Buying or Selling a Domain Name

. . . .

In This Chapter

▶ Avoiding some common buying pitfalls

▶ Identifying key selling problems

. . . .

*I*n many ways, buying or selling a domain name is a lot like buying or selling a piece of real estate. In both cases, there are precautions to take and pitfalls to avoid. In this chapter, we've compiled the top ten problems that people run into in the domain name resale market. By avoiding these common mistakes, you can help make sure that your experience in the domain name secondary market is a profitable and successful one.

Buying a Domain without Appraising Its Value

You wouldn't *think* of buying a house without having it inspected and appraised based on comparable sales. Likewise, you should never buy a domain name without getting an assessment of its fair market value. You can get a ballpark estimate of a domain name's market worth by following the steps in Chapter 10.

Buying a Domain Name That's Hard to Remember

A domain name that is too long, obscure, or difficult to spell will only make it harder for people to contact and do business with you. If you buy a tough-to-remember domain name, you'll end up spending a fair amount of time explaining or spelling it for people — time that you could much more profitably spend marketing and selling your products or services.

Buying a Country-Code Domain Name without Understanding the Requirements

More than 150 countries have their own country-code TLDs — suffixes such as .fr for France and .uk for the United Kingdom. Although some countries, such as the Cocos Islands, allow their ccTLDs to be registered and used by anyone, other nations have very strict rules that may require, for example, the owner of a ccTLD domain name to reside or do business within that country.

If you buy a ccTLD without understanding those special regulations in advance, you may end up with a domain name that you can't use or cannot own.

Neglecting to Stick to a Budget

Buying a domain name can be an impulsive, emotional decision. So setting a budget for your purchase ahead of time so that you know what you can really spend is important. If you have a budget in place and you find a domain name that you like, you'll be less likely to overpay or bust your budget in the heat of bidding or negotiations.

No matter how much you want a certain domain name, there are always others on the market that you may end up liking just as well.

Making a Purchase without Using an Escrow Service

If there is a cardinal rule about buying a domain name, this is it: Use an escrow service any time you purchase a domain name. If you don't use a neutral, professional, third-party escrow service to conclude the purchase transaction, you put yourself at risk in numerous ways. Without the verification process that an escrow company provides, you may find out — too late — that the seller is not really the registered owner. The seller may disappear with your money without transferring the name, or the owner may transfer it incorrectly.

Overpricing Your Domain Name When You're Ready to Sell

When it comes to domain names, a bird in the hand is definitely better than two that may (or may not) be in the bush. Selling your domain name for $5,000 is a whole lot better than letting it linger in the listings forever because you've priced it way too high. The fact is that overpriced names do not attract genuine buyers. Start by getting an accurate appraisal of your domain name's market value; then price it to sell.

Lying to a Potential Buyer about Other Offers

Misleading a potential buyer by claiming to have other offers when that is not the case is never a smart move. If the potential buyer finds out — which often happens — she may retaliate by dropping her offering price or by simply bolting from the deal.

Being Unavailable or Unresponsive

When you go to a store, nothing is more irritating than being ignored when you want to make a purchase. The same thing is true for buyers of domain names. If you're selling a name, make sure that you can be easily contacted. If you plan to be away, inform potential buyers so they're aware ahead of time. Like frustrated retail customers, domain name buyers — especially those in a hurry to make a deal — can easily change their minds and may end up taking their business elsewhere.

Dismissing an Offer

Every offer is worth looking at. Don't assume that a purchase inquiry isn't for real. Even if it seems like the offer isn't coming from a legitimate buyer, the source could actually be a foreign purchaser or a company that is trying to hide its true identity. Responding to and checking out the offer instead of dismissing it quickly out of hand is always a worthwhile strategy.

Selling a Domain Name without Using an Escrow Service

The golden rule of buying a domain name applies to selling one, too. Using an escrow service to conclude the sale transaction is the best way you can protect yourself against buyers who are illegitimate or who refuse to pay once the domain name has been transferred.

Chapter 21

Ten Domain Name Trademark Problems to Avoid

In This Chapter

▶ Recognizing the domain name trademark don'ts

▶ Avoiding trademark conflicts

*D*omain name trademark issues are especially important for anyone who intends to use their domain name commercially. This area of the law is far from black and white, but by avoiding some basic mistakes, you can reduce your risk of big problems later — from lawsuits and liabilities to the loss of your business domain name.

Cybersquatting

Cybersquatters are people who deliberately register the names of celebrities or the trademarks of famous companies who do not have a legitimate claim to the name, have no intent to use it, and hope to sell the names back to their rightful owners (or the highest bidder) for large amounts of money. Cybersquatters can be subject to legal penalties.

ICANN's Uniform Domain Name Dispute Resolution Policy focuses on disputes involving bad faith trademark issues. In addition, the Anticybersquatting Consumer Protection Act, passed by Congress in 1999, amends the Trademark Act of 1946 to enable trademark or service mark owners to sue, for civil damages, anyone who registers, traffics in, or uses a domain name with a bad faith intent to profit from the trademark.

A domain name holder who is found guilty of cybersquatting under the act may be ordered to forfeit or cancel the domain name or transfer it to the trademark owner. In addition, the guilty party may be liable for statutory damages ranging from $1,000 to $100,000 per domain name.

Trademark Infringement

Any unauthorized use of a trademarked name or mark may constitute *trademark infringement*. To win an infringement case, a trademark holder only needs to show that confusion is reasonably likely. Domain names can be — and have been — challenged for trademark infringement violations. If the holder of a domain name loses an infringement suit, he or she may be forced to forfeit the right to the name or may be barred from using it — an inconvenient and potentially costly situation, especially if goodwill has been established. The infringing party may also be found liable for damages sustained by the trademark holder.

Trademark Dilution

A domain name may cause a trademark dilution conflict if it dilutes or tarnishes the unique and distinctive qualities of a famous trademark or brand, such as Exxon or Coca-Cola. Famous trademarks are usually protected vigorously, so be sure to avoid registering any name that even *remotely* resembles a famous mark.

As a result, if you plan to use your domain name for business, it is very important to conduct a trademark search to make sure that the domain name is free of potential trademark conflicts. If you use a domain name that does have trademark conflicts, you could end up losing it or paying heavy fines to defend your right to keep it.

Neglecting to Do an Expanded State and Common-Law Trademark Search

If it looks like your domain name is free of trademark issues based on a preliminary search of federal marks, you should make certain by conducting a more comprehensive search of state and common-law trademarks. This type of search takes time and usually involves the help of a professional trademark specialist — but it is well worth taking this extra step if you plan to use your domain name for commercial purposes.

Not Trademarking Your Domain Name

After you have made sure that your domain name is clear of any potential trademark problems, the next move you should make is to protect it by applying for federal trademark registration.

Trademark registration is not required — you can establish common-law trademark rights by simply using your name in business. However, by registering your domain name as a federal trademark, you will increase your legal protections, including the legal presumption that you own the mark; exclusive rights to use the mark, according to its registration terms; the ability to bring a trademark infringement or dilution lawsuit in federal court; and the ability to ask the United States Customs Service to block the importation of infringing products. If you end up in a trademark dispute, the fact that your domain name is federally trademarked shifts the balance of legal presumptions in your favor.

Not Protecting Your Trademark

An additional move you should make to protect your domain name trademark rights is to monitor the marketplace for potential infringement of your mark. Several trademark monitoring companies can provide this service for you, including:

- **Cyveillance** (www.cyveillance.com), offering fee-based monthly intellectual property protection reporting.
- **NameProtect** (www.nameprotect.com), offering free NameGuard monthly Watch Reports on potential threats to your domain name.

Ignoring Global Trademark Issues

With the worldwide reach of the Internet, domain name trademark issues can be especially complex. Trademarks traditionally exist independently in each country in which they are registered, but these legal and physical borders break down on the Internet. Even though different countries have different trademark laws, domain names, by their very nature, cross international boundaries. As a result, the challenge of protecting and enforcing trademarks on the Internet is very complicated, and the mechanisms for doing so are still evolving. It is wise, at the very least, to be aware of potential international challenges to your domain name and to stay up-to-date as global dispute resolution standards develop.

Not Renewing Your Trademark

Federal trademarks are registered for ten-year periods, and they can be renewed for additional, unlimited ten-year terms as long as you continue to use the mark in commerce. A key point to remember is that after your federal trademark registration has been in effect for five years, you must file an "Affidavit of Use" providing certain required information — *before the sixth year* — or your registration will be canceled. At the end of your ten-year registration period, you must file to renew your federal trademark for another ten-year term. You have to submit this application *between the ninth and tenth year,* before your registration expires.

If you let your trademark registration lapse, you lose the protection that it provides. Moreover, you can lose your trademark if you fail to use it.

Not Getting Good Trademark Advice

If your domain name is challenged by the holder of a trademark for infringement, consult an attorney who has experience in trademark law. Only with good counsel can you determine whether someone is merely using "bully tactics" to take your domain name from you on thin grounds — or whether your challenger has a valid case. In either situation, you need good advice to determine your response and how you can best protect your domain name ownership.

Ignoring the Importance of Trademark Issues

If you are using your domain name in a business, you need to understand potential trademark problems and make sure that your domain name is free and clear of them. After all, if you are setting up a Web site and doing business on the Internet, you are investing a lot of your time and money. If later you lose your domain name in a trademark conflict, the damage to your business can be considerable. Trademark conflicts have become increasingly common, and many companies apply great legal pressure on domain name holders to enforce their rights. The better prepared and protected you are to begin with, the lower your chances of ending up in a potentially costly and damaging dispute.

Appendix A

A Guide to Global ccTLDs

• •

*R*egistering a domain name in the ccTLD of any country in which you do, or plan to do, business — such as `Myproduct.fr` (for France) or `Myproduct.co.uk` (for the United Kingdom) — is a good idea.

Following is a listing of all the available country codes, according to the Internet Assigned Numbers Authority. You need to get in touch with individual administrators to find out their national registration policies. Contact information for each ccTLD is available at the Internet Assigned Numbers Authority (IANA) Web site at `www.iana.org/cctld/cctld-whois.htm`.

ccTLD	*Country*
.ac	Ascension Island
.ad	Andorra
.ae	United Arab Emirates
.af	Afghanistan
.ag	Antigua and Barbuda
.ai	Anguilla
.al	Albania
.am	Armenia
.an	Netherlands Antilles
.ao	Angola
.aq	Antarctica
.ar	Argentina
.as	American Samoa
.at	Austria

(continued)

ccTLD	Country
.au	Australia
.aw	Aruba
.az	Azerbaijan
.ba	Bosnia and Herzegovina
.bb	Barbados
.bd	Bangladesh
.be	Belgium
.bf	Burkina Faso
.bg	Bulgaria
.bh	Bahrain
.bi	Burundi
.bj	Benin
.bm	Bermuda
.bn	Brunei
.bo	Bolivia
.br	Brazil
.bs	The Bahamas
.bt	Bhutan
.bv	Bouvet Island
.bw	Botswana
.by	Belarus
.bz	Belize
.ca	Canada
.cc	Cocos (Keeling) Islands
.cd	Democratic Republic of the Congo
.cf	Central African Republic
.cg	Republic of the Congo

ccTLD	Country
.ch	Switzerland
.ci	Cote d'Ivoire
.ck	Cook Islands
.cl	Chile
.cm	Cameroon
.cn	China
.co	Colombia
.cr	Costa Rica
.cu	Cuba
.cv	Cape Verde
.cx	Christmas Island
.cy	Cyprus
.cz	Czech Republic
.de	Germany
.dj	Djibouti
.dk	Denmark
.dm	Dominica
.do	Dominican Republic
.dz	Algeria
.ec	Ecuador
.ee	Estonia
.eg	Egypt
.eh	Western Sahara
.er	Eritrea
.es	Spain
.et	Ethiopia

(continued)

ccTLD	Country
.fi	Finland
.fj	Fiji
.fk	Falkland Islands (Islas Malvinas)
.fm	Federated States of Micronesia
.fo	Faroe Islands
.fr	France
.ga	Gabon
.gd	Grenada
.ge	Georgia
.gf	French Guiana
.gg	Guernsey
.gh	Ghana
.gi	Gibraltar
.gl	Greenland
.gm	The Gambia
.gn	Guinea
.gp	Guadeloupe
.gq	Equatorial Guinea
.gr	Greece
.gs	South Georgia and the South Sandwich Islands
.gt	Guatemala
.gu	Guam
.gw	Guinea-Bissau
.gy	Guyana
.hk	Hong Kong
.hm	Heard Island and McDonald Islands
.hn	Honduras

ccTLD	Country
.hr	Croatia
.ht	Haiti
.hu	Hungary
.id	Indonesia
.ie	Ireland
.il	Israel
.im	Isle of Man
.in	India
.io	British Indian Ocean Territory
.iq	Iraq
.ir	Iran
.is	Iceland
.it	Italy
.je	Jersey
.jm	Jamaica
.jo	Jordan
.jp	Japan
.ke	Kenya
.kg	Kyrgyzstan
.kh	Cambodia
.ki	Kiribati
.km	Comoros
.kn	Saint Kitts and Nevis
.kp	North Korea
.kr	South Korea
.kw	Kuwait
.ky	Cayman Islands

(continued)

ccTLD	Country
.kz	Kazakhstan
.la	Laos
.lb	Lebanon
.lc	Saint Lucia
.li	Liechtenstein
.lk	Sri Lanka
.lr	Liberia
.ls	Lesotho
.lt	Lithuania
.lu	Luxembourg
.lv	Latvia
.ly	Libya
.ma	Morocco
.mc	Monaco
.md	Moldova
.mg	Madagascar
.mh	Marshall Islands
.mk	The Former Yugoslav Republic of Macedonia
.ml	Mali
.mm	Myanmar
.mn	Mongolia
.mo	Macau
.mp	Northern Mariana Islands
.mq	Martinique
.mr	Mauritania
.ms	Montserrat
.mt	Malta

ccTLD	Country
.mu	Mauritius
.mv	Maldives
.mw	Malawi
.mx	Mexico
.my	Malaysia
.mz	Mozambique
.na	Namibia
.nc	New Caledonia
.ne	Niger
.nf	Norfolk Island
.ng	Nigeria
.ni	Nicaragua
.nl	Netherlands
.no	Norway
.np	Nepal
.nr	Nauru
.nu	Niue
.nz	New Zealand
.om	Oman
.pa	Panama
.pe	Peru
.pf	French Polynesia
.pg	Papua New Guinea
.ph	Philippines
.pk	Pakistan
.pl	Poland

(continued)

ccTLD	Country
.pm	Saint Pierre and Miquelon
.pn	Pitcairn Islands
.pr	Puerto Rico
.ps	Palestinian Territories
.pt	Portugal
.pw	Palau
.py	Paraguay
.qa	Qatar
.re	Reunion
.ro	Romania
.ru	Russia
.rw	Rwanda
.sa	Saudi Arabia
.sb	Solomon Islands
.sc	Seychelles
.sd	Sudan
.se	Sweden
.sg	Singapore
.sh	Saint Helena
.si	Slovenia
.sj	Svalbard and Jan Mayen
.sk	Slovakia
.sl	Sierra Leone
.sm	San Marino
.sn	Senegal
.so	Somalia
.sr	Suriname

ccTLD	Country
.st	Sao Tome and Principe
.sv	El Salvador
.sy	Syria
.sz	Swaziland
.tc	Turks and Caicos Islands
.td	Chad
.tf	French Southern and Antarctic Lands
.tg	Togo
.th	Thailand
.tj	Tajikistan
.tk	Tokelau
.tm	Turkmenistan
.tn	Tunisia
.to	Tonga
.tp	East Timor
.tr	Turkey
.tt	Trinidad and Tobago
.tv	Tuvalu
.tw	Taiwan
.tz	Tanzania
.ua	Ukraine
.ug	Uganda
.uk	United Kingdom
.um	U.S. Minor Outlying Islands
.us	United States
.uy	Uruguay

(continued)

ccTLD	*Country*
.uz	Uzbekistan
.va	Holy See (Vatican City)
.vc	Saint Vincent and the Grenadines
.ve	Venezuela
.vg	British Virgin Islands
.vi	Virgin Islands
.vn	Vietnam
.vu	Vanuatu
.wf	Wallis and Futuna
.ws	Western Samoa
.ye	Yemen
.yt	Mayotte
.yu	Yugoslavia
.za	South Africa
.zm	Zambia
.zr	Zaire
.zw	Zimbabwe

Appendix B

Glossary

● ●

*A*nticybersquatting Consumer Protection Act: Legislation passed by the U.S. Congress in 1999 to provide a remedy for victims of domain name cybersquatting. The act amends the Trademark Act of 1946 to enable trademark or service mark owners to sue, for civil damages, anyone who registers, traffics in, or uses a domain name with a bad faith intent to profit from the trademark.

ARPANET: Created in 1969 by the United States Defense Advanced Research Project Agency (ARPA), ARPANET was one of the first large computer networks connecting research centers and universities.

ccTLDs: Country-code TLDs, or domain name suffixes, linked to specific nations. The ccTLDs are based on the International Telecommunications Union codes for nations and territories worldwide. All ccTLDs are made up of two letters — for example, .us is the ccTLD for the United States, and .fr is the ccTLD for France.

clicks: The number of visits or hits that a Web site attracts.

cybersquatter: Someone who deliberately registers the domain names of celebrities or the trademarks of famous companies, denying the rightful owner access to the domain name in the hopes of selling it back to the owners (or the highest bidder) for large amounts of money.

Domain Name System (DNS): An Internet technology that translates domain names into their corresponding numerical IP (Internet Protocol) addresses.

extensions: Domain name suffixes, also called top-level domains (TLDs), that are used as categories for Internet addresses.

ftp: A code that informs the computer to use the file transfer protocol, the language used to send and download files over the Internet.

gopher: A code that instructs the computer to retrieve text-only information from the Web.

gTLDs: Generic TLDs (domain name suffixes) are available to anyone who wants a domain name for business, personal, or organizational use.

HTML: Short for *HyperText Markup Language,* used for creating documents to be posted on the World Wide Web.

http: Short for *HyperText Transfer Protocol;* it is a code that instructs the computer to retrieve a document on the World Wide Web.

ICANN: The Internet Corporation for Assigned Names and Numbers, a private sector, not-for-profit organization that administers policy for the Internet name and address system. ICANN was created as part of an effort to shift control of the Internet from the U.S. government to the international Internet community.

Internet: A decentralized network of millions of independent computers worldwide.

Internet Protocol (IP) address: A unique numerical identity code assigned to every computer on the Internet.

packet switching: A process that breaks information into discrete segments or *packets,* which are transmitted independently over the Internet, and then rejoins them when they reach their destination.

registrars: Retail companies that handle all consumer contact for domain name registrations, including customer service and billing.

registry administrators: Wholesale organizations around the world that maintain the master databases (called *root servers*) of all available domain names.

TCP/IP: Transmission control protocol/Internet protocol, the standard language used by computers on the Internet.

telnet: A protocol that enables you to access another computer over the Internet from a remote location.

TLDs: Top-level domains, or domain name suffixes, such as `.com`, `.net`, `.org`, and country-code TLDs.

trademark dilution: A form of trademark infringement in which a famous mark's unique and distinctive qualities are diluted or tarnished.

trademark infringement: Any unauthorized use of a trademarked name or mark.

URL: Uniform Resource Locator, the address of a document posted on the World Wide Web.

whois: A database that lists the registration and contact information for all domain name owners.

World Intellectual Property Organization (WIPO): An international forum accredited by ICANN to resolve global domain name trademark conflicts.

World Wide Web: A virtual network of documents and information connected by the authoring language called HTML, which enables users to point, click, and jump from one document or Web site to another.

Appendix C

Resources

● ●

*H*ere, at your fingertips, is an expanded list of useful domain-name-related Web sites, where you can find information on almost any subject related to Internet addresses. We've organized these recommended sites according to topic. From selecting and registering domain names to dispute resolution and trademark issues, the following Web sites will give you a wealth of helpful tips and ideas. Check the list, too, for useful sites when you're ready to buy, sell, or appraise a domain name property.

Selecting a Domain Name

You can find online thesauruses at:

- ✔ **Merriam-Webster, Inc.:** www.m-w.com/thesaurus.htm
- ✔ **Thesaurus.com:** www.thesaurus.com

Following are some sites with useful naming tools:

- ✔ **Domain Name Analyzer:** www.findgoodnames.com
- ✔ **IdeaFisher:** www.ideacenter.com
- ✔ **NameWave:** www.namestormers.com

These agencies provide domain naming services:

- ✔ **ABC Namebank:** www.abcnamebank.com
- ✔ **NameBase:** www.namebase.com
- ✔ **Name-It:** www.nameit.com
- ✔ **Namestormers:** www.namestormers.com
- ✔ **NameTrade:** www.nametrade.com

Registering Domain Names

Here are a variety of domain name registrars offering a range of features:

- **A+Net/ABACUS America, Inc.:** names4ever.com
- **Alldomains.com:** www.alldomains.com
- **BulkRegister.com, Inc.:** www.bulkregister.com
- **Catalog.com Inc.:** www.catalog.com
- **Domain Registration Services:** www.dotearth.com
- **DomainRegistry.com:** www.domainregistry.com
- **DomainZoo.com, Inc.:** www.domainzoo.com
- **DotRegistrar.com:** www.dotregistrar.com
- **Dotster, Inc.:** www.dotster.com
- **Easyspace Ltd.:** www.easyspace.com
- **e-names.org:** www.e-names.org
- **EnetRegistry.com Corporation:** www.enetregistry.com
- **eNom, Inc.:** www.enom.com
- **FirstDomain.net:** www.firstdomain.net
- **Global Knowledge Group:** www.gkg.net
- **Internet Domain Registrars:** www.registrars.com
- **ItsYourDomain.com:** www.itsyourdomain.com
- **The NameIt Corporation:** nameit.net
- **NameSecure.com:** www.namesecure.com
- **Network Solutions:** www.networksolutions.com
- **Parava Networks:** www.naame.com
- **register.com:** www.register.com
- **The Registry at InfoAvenue:** www.iaregistry.com
- **Signature Domains, Inc.:** www.signaturedomains.com
- **Speednames, Inc.:** www.speednames.com
- **Stargate Communications, Inc.:** www.stargateinc.com
- **TierraNet Inc.:** www.domaindiscover.com

Domain Name Dispute Resolution

These organizations provide ICANN-accredited domain name dispute resolution services:

- **CPR Institute for Dispute Resolution:** www.cpradr.org
- **Disputes.org/eResolution Consortium (eResolution):** www.eresolution.ca
- **The National Arbitration Forum:** www.arbforum.com
- **World Intellectual Property Organization:** arbiter.wipo.int

Domain Name Trademark Issues

The following sites offer information and resources regarding trademark matters:

- **1-2-3 Trademark:** www.1-2-3-trademark.com
- **4TradeMark.com:** www.trademark-search.com
- **Cyveillance:** www.cyveillance.com
- **International Trademark Association (INTA):** www.inta.org
- **MarksOnline:** www.marksonline.com
- **NameProtect:** www.nameprotect.com
- **The Sunnyvale Center on Innovation, Invention and Ideas:** www.sci3.com
- **Thomson & Thomson:** www.thomson-thomson.com
- **Trademark Center:** www.tmcenter.com
- **Trademark Express:** www.tmexpress.com
- **U.S. Patent and Trademark Office:** www.uspto.gov

Escrow Services

You can obtain escrow services for domain name sales and purchases at sites including:

- **Escrow.com:** www.escrow.com
- **GreatDomains:** www.greatdomains.com
- **Tradenable:** www.tradenable.com

Domain Name Listing Services

Dozens of domain name listing services and brokers are available on the Web. They include:

- **ABCOM Domain Name Resales:** www.fastprofits.net
- **AllFreeDomains.com:** www.allfreedomains.com
- **ComBuys.com:** www.combuys.com
- **DomainBook.com:** www.domainbook.com
- **DomainRealtor.com:** www.domainrealtor.com
- **eDomainRealty.com:** www.edomainrealty.com
- **GreatDomains:** www.greatdomains.com
- **MightyDomains.com:** www.mightydomains.com/sell.htm
- **TargetDomain:** www.targetdomain.com
- **TheDomainEmporium.com:** www.thedomainemporium.com
- **Time2Sell:** www.time2sell.com
- **URL Resources:** www.urlresources.com

Domain Name Auction Sites

Domain name resale auctions are held at many Web sites, including the following:

- **Afternic:** www.afternic.com
- **Choicefree:** www.choicefree.com
- **eBay:** listings.ebay.com/aw/listings/list/all/category3767
- **HitDomains:** www.solutionhome.com
- **NamesForBid.com:** www.namesforbid.com
- **ShoutLoud.com:** www.shoutloud.com
- **TheDomainAuction.com:** www.thedomainauction.com
- **Yahoo! Auctions:** auctions.yahoo.com/27751-category-leaf.html

Domain Name Appraisals

You can have your domain name valued at sites including:

- ✔ **DomainiQ:** www.domainiq.com/appraisals.htm
- ✔ **Domain Systems:** www.solutionhome.com/appraisal
- ✔ **DomainActions.com:** www.domainactions.com
- ✔ **DomainAppraise.com:** www.domainappraise.com
- ✔ **GreatDomains.com:** www.greatdomains.com/services/appraisal/appraisalinfo.asp
- ✔ **honestdomains:** www.honestdomains.com/appraise.htm
- ✔ **WebmasterExpert:** www.webmasterexpert.com/domainappraise.htm

Index

FOR DUMMIES
BOOK REGISTRATION

Register This Book and Win!

We want to hear from you!

Visit **dummies.com** to register this book and tell us how you liked it!

- ✔ Get entered in our monthly prize giveaway.

- ✔ Give us feedback about this book — tell us what you like best, what you like least, or maybe what you'd like to ask the author and us to change!

- ✔ Let us know any other *For Dummies* topics that interest you.

Your feedback helps us determine what books to publish, tells us what coverage to add as we revise our books, and lets us know whether we're meeting your needs as a *For Dummies* reader. You're our most valuable resource, and what you have to say is important to us!

Not on the Web yet? It's easy to get started with *Dummies 101: The Internet For Windows 98* or *The Internet For Dummies* at local retailers everywhere.

Or let us know what you think by sending us a letter at the following address:

For Dummies Book Registration
Dummies Press
10475 Crosspoint Blvd.
Indianapolis, IN 46256

™

BESTSELLING BOOK SERIES